MW01593225

Buying Wealth With Money

The Temple Of Light Publishing
www.thetempleoflight.com

ISBN: 978-1-949311-11-2
www.emotionalmanagement.org

**AI will never be used in my work.
Support artists, not machines.**

Artwork in order of appearance:

But Who Has Won? Alice In Wonderland, by Arthur Rackham
The Stone Pickers, by George Clausen
The Sword Of Damocles, by Wenceslas Hollar
Jesus Drives Out The Money-Changers, by Alexandre Bida
Alone, by Jozef Israëls
Ant & Grasshopper, an illustration from *The Fables of Aesop*, by Jacobs
The Cicada And The Ant, by Gustave Doré
Blasts Of The Ram's Horn book illustration, by Frank Beard
King Midas With His Daughter, by Arthur Rackham
The Blind Girl, by John Everett Millais
The Lovers, by Saktiawan

Characters: None of the names or people portrayed or referenced in this work, unless noted, are based on fictional or non-fictional people, animals, places, or events, and any similarity is accidental. "Only the gods are real."

Table Of Contents

*"I'd like to live as a poor man
with lots of money."*
-Pablo Picasso

If Someone Gave You This Book

*Y*ou were given this workbook because sharing what we love or helps us love is absolute kindness. May you receive this workbook in the same spirit it was given: Kindness.

This is not a "you're worse than me at life, so here is a handout." No. We all struggle, and neither I nor the giver of this book is any better or worse than you. I wish I had these tools decades ago—you are holding this book because the person who gave it to you believes in you.

And so do I.

We both think—no … we both *know* that we can all improve our lives and that this is the most wonderful gift we could ever give ourselves and others. From letting go of past anger to finding your passions, there is more to this workbook than its title, just as there is so much more to you than your name or past.

And so I close before beginning by saying what I would if we were face-to-face:

Welcome, dear brother / sweet sister. Welcome! Let's let go of being victims and villains. Let's grow together and become the heroes this world so desperately needs.

—Raven

Preface

One of the best pieces of advice on relationships was given to me by someone who was not in a relationship. Similarly, many poor people have given me the best advice on money, which is simply, "Live below your means."

Each book in this series, originally workbooks on emotional management, is a continuation of the first book: *Hero, Vol. 1, Drafting Your Hero & Villain*.

> *"Don't be pushed around by the fears in your mind.*
> *Be led by the dreams in your heart."*
> *-Roy T. Bennett*

Why tell you this?

It is difficult to be a hero when you cannot help anyone because you have not yet helped yourself. And who knows what battles you may still face?

It is time to be able to help those in need.

It is time to be a hero.

> *"He attacked everything in life with a mix of*
> *extraordinary genius and naïve incompetence,*
> *and it was often difficult to tell which was which."*
> *-Douglas Adams*

Introduction

Of all the things I was told not to write on, this was number one—not by others, but by myself.

Writing about giving money to charities you love? Oh, that is easy and welcomed by all. But if I dared speak on how to make that money to begin with, I would be labeled a sellout before my first printing. Yet, name the hero who cannot afford to buy a maiden her meal, or a knight his needed steel!

To be a hero, we must move forward. From no longer being undone by fears to achieving our goals, from better relationships to improving the chance of having one at all, life is better when you strengthen yourself.

This book will help you make money.
This series will help you become wealthy.

Money is cash. It can be gambled, spent on frivolous things, or stolen.

Wealth is love. We can give our time only if we have time. We can fund only if we have funds. If I can help courageous and heroic hearts not only give, but give more, then I have achieved all I have set out to do.

"Live like a hero.
That's what the classics teach us.
Be a main character. Otherwise, what is life for?"
-J.M. Coetzee

— Hero, Vol. 4: Opening —

This is taboo.
This is *so* taboo!

I mean, you cannot say what I am about to say.

Ladies and Gentlemen, the truth is:
Money can buy happiness.

Wait!

If you think it cannot, then, unlike me, you have never been homeless. I've gone without food many times, and I have been cold but too poor to turn on the heat. When your mother is without food or needs medicine, I assure you, money buys happiness.

In this, I want good people to have wealth, and plenty of it, for two quick reasons:
The best way to make money is to provide value.
And valuable people often take some of that reward and use it to lift others up.
What the world needs is not a million people in rags who want to help, but millions of people who can. That is why this section is so important.

This is not one of those "do this then that" types of lists. These steps will need to be revisited often. Yet, the principles herein have taken me from homelessness to living a good life (and I'll continue to work towards making it even better). These steps can also guide you, no matter where you are in life, not to where I want to be, but where you want to be. But only if you treat this workbook as important.

Write the answers.

<u>Underline important points.</u>

Apply all the steps. (Action!)

No!

Actually do all of that.

Why?

If you do, then you will succeed.

What does that mean?

It means everyone will be blessed because you do. And that, if nothing more, makes a man or woman a hero.

Let's begin.

Let's Make A Deal

If you apply everything herein, it will work. And where you are right now doesn't matter; you can do this if you are homeless or run many companies. This will work! But I have one request:

If I gave you a hundred dollar bill, would you, in return, give ten dollars back?

Here is the deal: Once you apply everything, give 10% of that increased income to a charity you love.

Does that sound fair?

Then let's get started.

"Wealth after all is a relative thing
since he that has little and wants less
is richer than he that has much and wants more."
-Charles Caleb Colton

What Is Enough?

𝒟ecades ago, I saw something that changed my life. The problem is it took me decades to let it.

"Courage is the first of human qualities because it is the quality which guarantees the others."
-Winston Churchill

Above the stage was a projected graph—just a huge square with numbers and a jagged red line going up, but what it represented caught my eye. It was a worldwide study on wealth and happiness. No surprise that zero income had the lowest overall happiness. Now, you can be poor and still be kind and smile, but you are not happy if you cannot provide healthy food, let alone food, for your children or yourself.

There was a sharp increase in happiness at the $25,000 mark. Then the line gradually leveled out until it reached $64,000. This did not surprise me. What did was the difference in overall happiness between people who had $64,000 a year and those who had over $1,000,000. The increase was so small it was practically indistinguishable! There was almost no enhancement in joy.

Times have changed. Money's value has been altered and currencies differ, but not as much as people. The first step to having financial well-being, whether you are single, in a relationship, or recovering from a loss is to determine the level of income needed to bring you to a place of peace.

Two types will have problems with this. One is too greedy, and the other thinks being wealthy makes them less able to show virtue, rather than more able to be virtuous. But, if you are honest throughout this workbook, these steps will improve your life and the lives of those around you—provided you do not wait decades to apply them!

Many say they want a million per year, yet have no idea why. Just saying you want a million dollars doesn't mean anything, but if you say, "I need $240,000 a year to be at my happiest" now I know, and you know, that you have done the math. You have your *why*.

> *"Being rich is not about how much money you have or how many homes you own; it's the freedom to buy any book you want without looking at the price and wondering if you can afford it."*
> *-John Waters*

Housing:

It is easy to get caught up in fantasy or denial. If you go with fantasy, and say you need a billion dollars so you can have a castle, then no problem! None! Let's look at it: Do you want to live there all the time, or do you want to travel a lot? If you want to travel for many months out of the year, then instead of owning one castle, you could experience many castles throughout the year by staying at them on your journeys. Even if it costs thousands per stay, it is not only cheaper than billions, but you get to enjoy dozens of castles, instead of just one.

Or say you went into denial and claimed you only want rent money—no problem! None! Let's look at it: Would a nicer place to rent help you as an artist, as a host for dinner guests or family, or to provide a better home for your dog? Let's also say you want to travel one month out of the year; then we need to add rent for that month both at home and where you travel.

A free cardboard box will not provide as much joy as a decent place to co-rent, and that will not provide as much joy as a nice home in the country. Would a million-dollar mansion increase your joy as much as it would from zero (cardboard box level of happiness) to that of a decent home (mid-level)? What about your dream farm (high-level)? Is that fancy house nothing more than social proof (no increased happiness level)?

There always comes a point of diminishing returns, so aim for where you think true happiness rests. Would a billion-dollar castle really bring more happiness than an apartment overlooking the city you love, a small farm in the country, or a humble home with great neighbors, family, and friends who live nearby?

Being honest about this can be scary, but consider it carefully, and do the math many times without worrying about the amount of money. The number is simply a number, after all, and it won't hurt you. Calculate your total for the year and write it below.

Housing: $_____

*"Too many people spend money they haven't earned,
to buy things they don't want,
to impress people that they don't like."*
-Will Rogers

Travel:

Plane tickets, fuel, and the like? Absolutely. Many items on this list overlap, so you'll need to tweak them as you go. We covered renting places to stay and we will get to vehicle expenses, but will you need additional insurance when you travel or are you already fully covered? That is why the first few walkthroughs of this will be a rough draft, and that is okay. It will come together in the end.

How many places do you want to travel to? Don't answer based on whether you think you could afford it or would have the time. Where would you genuinely love to go? Are there 100 places? Or is it 78? Or maybe there are 10 places you really want to visit, but once you do, the 20 places you kind of want to see get either pushed aside for those 10—or those 10 were so epic that now you have to see 300 new places because who knows what you might discover? Will you hire a translator, or will you learn the language first? There are certainly many options.

This list will change year to year, but for now, what do you think is an honest estimate of the funds you would need annually to fully enjoy travel?

Travel: $_____

"If you say that getting the money is the most important thing, you'll spend your life completely wasting your time. You'll be doing things you don't like doing in order to go on living, that is to go on doing things you don't like doing, which is stupid."
-Alan Watts

Food:

Think about it as if money were no object. That doesn't mean fancy food you wouldn't want anyway or even more junk food. If given whatever they wanted for food, some would swiftly become unhealthy. If the bar poured drinks for free, hundreds of thousands of people would be dead by the end of a month. Instead, embrace your self-worth and how much you love others, and answer this the way your future self would—the you of today, after all, no longer enjoys the junk food you consumed (and were consumed by) last year. Instead, consider food in ways you may not have before:

What would it cost to hire a chef to come in twice a week and make healthy food? We don't need a fancy restaurant for every meal, but we also shouldn't limit our thoughts to only junk food. We cannot operate at our heroic best while consuming the worst. Food is important. Food is information.

You need quality food for mental and physical fuel to drive you forward. Not energy drinks and snacks, but purple sweet potatoes, black rice, and lentils—not only greens from a victory garden, but reds, oranges, yellows, and every color you can find. If you shortchange your mind and health, it will never lead to wealth—only more medical bills. Aim to eat healthier than anyone you know. Indeed, you should not even be able to imagine how you could eat any healthier. To do this, and do it easily, be sure to read *Hero, Vol. 2*.

Look at the best places to buy food and see what the best food would cost. Figure up a month's worth of food costs, including any times you want to buy dinner for others, tips, hosting family, or extra costs while traveling. Then total it up, round it up a little to make sure, and write the yearly cost.

Food: $_____

Clothing:

Would having 20 outfits you thoroughly enjoy bring more or less happiness than having only one? Would owning thousands of shirts actually bring you 10% more joy than a hundred? Are you sure?

A few years ago, I would have found this section silly. I might have spent $100 on clothing a year—tops! Now? I hire seamstresses to make Nordic attire and each piece costs that much, if not three times more.

If a lack of money was not holding you back, what would you like to wear? Would your linen shorts be organic, made in the USA, and perfectly tailored instead of bothering you because they gape in the back? And what about your watch? No one needs to spend silly amounts, but what if you want a silver pocket watch or a jewel instead?

Some people avoid nice clothes because they think they don't deserve them or it would mean they are vain. Others want a dress with diamonds all over it, not because it is pretty, but because it shows off money. Focus, not on what others think, but on how you would feel wearing nice clothes. Guilt and greed are equally unhealthy. Is this how you would like to dress when alone? If someone showed up, would they compliment your attire because it's authentically you, or because it costs a lot? Self-honesty is not easy, but this is worth it, so take your time. What would you spend each year?

Clothing: $_____

"Price is what you pay.
Value is what you get."
-Warren Buffett

16

Vehicles:

Do you want a car, or two cars and a motorcycle? Did you immediately think of a fancy car that costs half a million? What does one of those cost if it is used? $125,000? Can you drive two cars at once? Do you really need them, or would you always worry about your car when parking downtown at your favorite restaurant? What would it cost to rent one of these cool cars for a week instead? Your first thought of half a million for a car might shift to something like: $12,000 for a nice used car, $3,000 to rent fancy vehicles occasionally, and $4,000 for maintenance and insurance: $19,000. Since the car should last five or so years, and you probably would only rent a fancy car once, with some costs not reoccurring, your annual expense year may actually be $8,000 or less.

Write the total cost, and do not shortchange yourself. If you want a specific vehicle, include it along with the cost. This is the only fair thing to do. For me, I have always wanted a motorcycle with a sidecar, so I included the average cost of a quality used one on my list. If you want a truck with a supercharger, that is not strange—it is simply what you want, so write the truth:

Vehicles: $_____

> *"Money is a great servant but a bad master."*
> *-Francis Bacon*

Donations / Charity / Family:

Now, yes, I would love to have trillions upon trillions and hire people to identify needs I could throw money at all day. Indeed, this might be the hardest one of all to imagine.

Over the last five years, how have you wished you could help? Was there a fundraiser for a dog and cat rescue where you would have loved to buy an auction item as a gift and to help them out? Have you ever wished you could have sent a friend a homemade blanket purchased from the ladies at church? Your story is, of course, your own.

Once a year, I buy blankets and bags made from worn-out saris bought at a fair price from poor people on the street—and they are given a new outfit, too! These are then sewn by individuals who have been rescued from prostitution; the earnings provide them with a safe place to live, a good wage, and medical care for themselves and their children. I then joyfully give these away as gifts to different people each year. Many of our purchases can be made in ways that help others. From fundraisers to auction sites where sellers donate part of the sale, you can find clothing or handcrafted items your aunts and uncles would adore. Find ways to double or triple the impact of your charity.

Reflect on the last few years—what would have been an average you would have liked to give? It does not need to be the biggest number on this list for you to have a generous heart. Once more, the number is irrelevant, but the honesty of your heart is not.

Giving: $_____

Entertainment:

Concerts, artwork, music, plays, festivals, and what you may spend there are all things to consider. Do you go to the museum? Would you like to? Do you enjoy playing cards? What if you had a nice poker table? Or are sports your thing? We all need some enjoyment, and while this is not the main reason for wealth (and can even be the downfall of it or what prevents you from building it in the first place), it is fair to enjoy enjoyments. Let entertainment be one of your joys— not an addiction or something that distracts you from family, friends, or pursuits.

Don't aim for what you think you want; instead, aim for what would enrich your life, your family, friends, and community. Consider this playfully in your imagination, such as hot air balloon rides to white water rafting, seeing a ballet performance to a huge concert, or even hosting your own festival or parties. What would you like to be able to spend on entertainment for yourself and friends?

Entertainment: $_____

"It isn't clear to me that giving people money actually solves the problem of poverty. Because poverty is very much more complex than the mere lack of money, even though that is a cardinal element of poverty."
-Dr. Jordan Peterson

Investments In Self:

Some see every video course or book set as a scam (and some are), but investing in yourself is a practice of self-improvement that holds limitless value. I have read books on emotional management that I would empty my bank account to send to a younger self. I'd pay it all! There is information out there, both for your personal struggles and passions, that *will* reduce your hardships and amplify your joys. If you like painting, buy the best books on art, a few video courses, and sign up for live classes. Invest in yourself! You are worth it. And what hero is not highly skilled in their craft, and well fortified against their weaknesses (villains)? In my not-so-humble opinion, this number should never be less than 5% of your earnings, and probably 10% or more.

Investment In Self: $_____

Personally Yours:

Sticking with art, how much do your paints cost? Or do you play the piano? Tuning it isn't free. And bigger still? Do you have, or are you planning on having a child? How much will their travel, food, health care, and education cost? Or maybe you have a victory garden? Tools, mulch, composts, and seeds add up. What is in your life today or next year? While these things bring joy, they do cost. Consider it and pay no mind to the number. It is, once more, just a number.

Personally Yours: $_____

"You'd be surprised what people will do for money that they wouldn't do for love."
-Rachel Caine

Savings:

Living paycheck to paycheck is stressful. How much do you need in savings to feel secure? Is it enough to live off for a year (based solely on needs, not wants)? Saving back enough to ensure you are not endangering yourself or your family is essential for keeping villainous times at bay. Yet, most put savings at the bottom of their list. "I'll start saving once I buy this, have that, and am making this amount or more." No! You have to do it now! Make it a game, a fun challenge, and a point of honor to save a set percentage each month. And this amount should remain untouched. If you need $25,000 in your savings to feel secure, and you have $25,001, then you have one dollar. That's it. The rest is sacred and not to be touched unless there is a true emergency. And define what that is! A "deal" on an item is not an emergency.

You cannot control abundance if you cannot thrive in scarcity. Many buy all they can, not all they need. Paying yourself 10% is a good place to start. Most banks can even make this automatic for you. Vow that from henceforth, you will put a set percentage into savings each month. If you do not have enough money to save any, sell your belongings and go door to door looking for work to make enough.

Monthly percentage to be put in savings: ___%

Savings needed: $_____

"If you've got a dollar and you spend 29 cents on a loaf of bread, you've got 71 cents left; But if you've got seventeen grand and you spend 29 cents on a loaf of bread, you've still got seventeen grand. There's a math lesson for you."
-Steve Martin

Necessities & Nonsense:

How much is your phone bill, or updating your computer to one you'd prefer? What about the cost of soap, toiletries, a washing machine, and the like? This list can often get absurdly long or miss essential things. Take a mental stroll through all your spaces, be it your place of worship or exercise: Do you tithe 10%? Does the gym cost $70 a month, but you spend $5 at their café daily? How much will insurance cost if you live the way you want or make the amount you want to make? This list will have to be revisited.

Necessities & Nonsense: $_____

"We are all self-made,
but only the successful will admit it."
-Earl Nightingale

Other:

Time to stretch your imagination. What about a hot-air balloon ride, a massage, acupuncture, or a bicycle? Wouldn't it be awesome to invest in an iron supplement? There is a Russian one that combats weakness like no other—they are called kettlebells. Or what about your pet? Wouldn't it be nice if your cat ate better? No. Even better than that. And wouldn't a nice bed be good for him, or would that be settled if you just gave in and put a sheet on the couch and let the cat win that one? It is, after all, just a couch. Speaking of beds, what about your bed or pillow?

Other: $_____

Total of all the above lines: $_____

> *"Lottery: A tax on people who are bad at math."*
> *-Ambrose Bierce*

Taxes:

Income tax, bills, debts, and fines—oh, my! How much would you have to earn to have the total left over after paying self-employment taxes? And add all debts up and figure out a reasonable amount to pay each year (20% of all income is a good starting point). What about business expenses that cannot be written off on your taxes? Add these up:

Taxes: $_____

Add Taxes and Total: $_____

That's what your best life would cost.

If you already make that amount or more, begin delegating so you can pursue time with charities and family and focus more on your passions.

If that number seems scary, divide it by 365 to see what it is per day. People do make that much per day.

Daily total: $_____

> *"Don't wait for something outside of yourself*
> *to make you happy in the future. Think how*
> *really precious is the time you have to spend,*
> *whether it's at work or with your family.*
> *Every minute should be enjoyed and savored."*
> *-Earl Nightingale*

Desired Time

I'd rather be smiling while living in my car than crying and depressed in a million-dollar home. Then again, I'd rather be smiling in a nice home than smiling while living in a car.

That said, you now have the amount that is best for you. It is no longer, "I wish I had a million dollars a year." It is, "My emotions are my choice, but the life I truly want costs: $_____."

But there is more. How much time off, and in what way, do you need to enjoy a meaningful life? Some people try to say they need 365 days off a year, leaving them to work one day on leap years, but that does not provide a sense of purpose. Yet, would three-day weekends be better for you than one? Maybe it would be better to work for six months and then play for six months.

Without trying to make this fit your current job, what work-to-enjoyment ratio would be best for you? I know people who would go stark raving mad (why is it always *stark raving mad* and not just *unhappy*, but I digress) if they had to take three days off a month. It would be unbearable. Others, if they had to work six days a week—well, they would choose homelessness over that. So this is your call. Not mine. Not society's.

This will change. If you can grow to love your work, then working 80 hours a week could be as enjoyable as vacations! But, for now, give an estimate. Write in hours per week or weeks a year, or however you prefer:

Time to work: _____

Time to play: _____

Where You Are

If you want to go to Denver but do not know where you are, you cannot even begin. Do you need a bus or a plane ticket? Can you walk or are there layovers? And Denver is huge! Where exactly in Denver do you want to go? Without knowing where you are, a map is irrelevant. Learning how to make and manage money doesn't matter if you do not know what you are making now. How much do you make per year after taxes?

$_____

Per day is: $_____

How much did your household spend last year on all the previous (housing, food, etc.)?

$_____

Per day is: $_____

Time spent working? _____

Time spent in enjoyable adventure? _____

It is easier to dream of where we want to be than to acknowledge where we are. But if we do not know, we cannot grow. It is as simple as that. I know it takes time, but figure out the above before continuing.

Buying Time &
Time Management Basics

ᴴave you heard the cliché that money doesn't buy time? That is as much of a lie as "money doesn't buy happiness."

"Annual income twenty pounds, annual expenditure nineteen and six, result happiness. Annual income twenty pounds, annual expenditure twenty pounds ought and six, result misery."
-Charles Dickens

The first step in this strange shopping experience is to determine what your time is worth. Add up the time you spend working for money in a week, including the hours clocked in, the time spent commuting, and any prep or cleaning up you have to do afterward. Then take the after-tax income, and divide it by the total number of hours worked. This is your real hourly wage. Do not guess. Take time to figure this out down to the penny:

My real hourly wage: $_____.____

Is that what you are worth? No. But your time is currently being sold for that. Yet, as an aside, there is another "buyer" we often overlook. We know the government takes money from our paychecks, but we also need to consider that our cars, housing, clothing, food, and the like, also claim portions of our paychecks. This leaves us with our actual net income. In this, many work full-time jobs just to make five dollars a month.

Your real hourly wage is not what you will be worth in the future. If you drink a lot, that number will go down (even if the digits go up; the purchasing power will not be the same). On the other hand, if you keep studying and striving forward and growing, that number will increase, but we are not focused on that just yet.

"Don't let the fear of the time it will take to accomplish something stand in the way of your doing it. The time will pass anyway; we might just as well put that passing time to the best possible use."
-Earl Nightingale

Let's say you thought you were worth $18 an hour, but after taxes and time, you just found out you are worth $12.51 an hour. No problem. Let's use that money to buy some time.

You change your own oil. Fair enough. Once you add up the cost of the oil, disposal fees, towels, filter, and the little bit of added coolant, brake fluid, and windshield wiper fluid, it costs $39.50 and an hour of your time. The shop on your way to work charges $48.53 after tax and has you in and out of there in 15-16 minutes. Plus they vacuum your car and clean your windows—you forgot to add that to your time. During that time, you could read about your passions, which will increase your future income.

With your time included, changing the oil yourself costs $12.51 + $39.50 = $52.01 to change your oil. Adding a fourth of the time to the car shop costs $3.13 + $48.53 = $51.66. It is cheaper, even at a low wage, to hire someone else to change your oil for you. And you were going to be reading that book anyway, so no need to add your time to the last equation.

Let's look once more, but this time we will make it easier. Let's say you are making $53.44 an hour, and you can hire someone to do your laundry, dishes, housecleaning, and even cooking for $22.00 an hour. Well now, that math just got way simpler, didn't it?

"Only the educated are free."
-Epictetus

Instead of spending 20 hours a week doing these tasks (taxes, yard work, or the like), you can hire someone else to do this job for less—sometimes much less than the time you spend on it yourself. And the time you save, the time you buy back? Spend it making more money? Sure. Spend it bettering yourself? Absolutely. Spend it with your daughter and son? That is something you never want to pay someone else to do unless absolutely necessary and only with deeply trusted caregivers (plural for your kid's safety). You can buy time, but, once you do, don't waste it on frivolous activities, nor sell off what is important (pets, family, friends, or passions) for what is only temporary (time traded for money). Why? Because money can buy wealth but is not wealth itself.

Buying time gives you more time for greater things, while wasting time robs life of greater joys. So consider: How much does a movie actually cost? Figure up how much time you pay to commute, and watch it, as well as the time it took to earn the money to pay for the movies on Friday night, drinking Saturday night, and video games on Sunday night. What is that in hours? What could you gain from this instead? And what might you lose in addition if things go poorly, such as being arrested for drunk driving, even though you only had a couple of drinks? At present, that is a minimum loss of

$30,000, and that is *if* you get to keep your job, let alone the possibility of losing family members, friends, and the respect of loved ones or even yourself. More? What if the woman you were meant to meet never crossed your path because you were playing video games? Or the man of your dreams was walking his dog while you were at the films and your dog was in a cage?

I am not saying to never see a film, play games, or to live in a state of fear of missing out. I am saying to treat treats as treats, not pseudo-treatments for boredom. Find three ways—do the math and make the plan—to buy time:

1.

2.

3.

*"People who have goals succeed
because they know where they're going.
It's that simple."*
-Earl Nightingale

When having a conversation with a date, taking a walk in nature, or trying to write music, small distractions cause large deficits in joy and reduce the full utilization of time spent.

Consider a couple on a date. He looks at his phone, then, a few minutes later, she checks hers. They both pull out their phones to take a picture, then she gets a call, and, while she is distracted, he texts to distract himself. Maybe this takes place over two hours, but how long between these times does it take before full attention is on the other person? Or was it ever?

When you rest, rest. Don't dabble in work.
When you work, work. Don't dabble in rest.
When you are with someone, be with someone.

We've all seen people "taking a break" at work while talking about work, arranging things, checking their email, and not even noticing if the food they're eating tastes good. This same type of person talks to coworkers about weekend plans while working. This multitasking doesn't automatically switch off, and, as a result, we are not present even with a partner, child, or at that festival we've been talking about all week. Our minds wander because we have allotted all things to all times, rather than dedicating specific times for each.

"The best way to predict your future is to create it."
-Peter Drucker

Could you set aside time for distractions you want to keep? Write 10 things that sidetrack you (e-mail, noise, or even talking to yourself).

1.
2.
3.
4.
5.
6.
7.
8.
9.
10.

What are three of the most beneficial things you do to nurture who you are?

1.
2.
3.

What are three of the worst things you do that inhibit who you want to become?

1.
2.
3.

If you cut out some wasted time from the evening, went to bed a little earlier, and woke up a little sooner, could you gain more time for self-improvement? Even by adding 30 minutes to your pursuit each morning, how much additional joy could you experience in a month? What about a year? What about 10 years? Play with some math on the sides of this page, and then make a plan to implement these ideas.

What would you gain by doing this?

What would not doing this provide?

In the movie *What About Bob*, Bob (Bill Murray) receives the most help of all, not from the therapist (Richard Dreyfus), but from the title of the doctor's book called *Baby Steps*. In time management, baby steps are critical. By removing what holds you back, and doing a little more of what you love, you can increase your joy.

"Rich people have small TVs and big libraries,
and poor people have small libraries and big TVs."
-Zig Ziglar

Not having time to show love, complete projects, or pursue passions adds stress to our relationships. From businesses to personal time, many triple their productivity and enjoyment through time management. Even if all you gain is 10% less stress and 20% more time you enjoy, taking *baby steps* is worth it.

"Success is the progressive realization
of a worthy goal or ideal."
-Earl Nightingale

They all ran around in circles, racing aimlessly.
"But who has won?" asked Alice.
[The runners pause, scratch their heads, and wonder].

Finding & Honing Your Passions

Long ago, before I was even five, I discovered my passions: the martial arts (Ninjutsu, Tae Kwon Do, and, later in life, Tai Chi Chuan and dance), story (in writing and philosophical tales), wildlife (animal husbandry), and tending the garden of Earth, our only Eden (and later I was drawn to grapevines and a viticulturist was born). In each of these pursuits, instructing is at the core of who I am.

But that is me.

How do you find your passions?

Look back to your youth. Your passion is there. Hidden or in plain sight. Did you like oboe music? Did you draw a picture for the fridge once a year or five times a day? Were you praised for bringing in pretty flowers? Would you watch the bees for hours on end?

Granted, I was a lucky one. I grew up on a farm, and, even as a youngster, my time in town was at the library. You may have grown up on video games and shows, but you can still sit in meditation and reflect on what has drawn you in, even if only a bit more than other things. And if not, maybe spend time in nature and perusing vast libraries.

"You have to be burning with an idea, or a problem, or a wrong that you want to right. If you're not passionate enough from the start, you'll never stick it out."
-Steve Jobs

Three things make someone great at a profession, and in providing above-average value through solving tougher problems, success and wealth can arise. But you must have:

1. Natural Talent

Being gifted does not mean you play *Moonlight Sonata* your first time at a piano. It means you have an inborn desire to play. A child who does not want to learn something, will not; the same child, if she wants to learn something, will. If she has no interest in math, no one can teach her with any ease, and she will swiftly forget. Yet, if she loves learning new words, she will pick them up with the greatest of ease and retain them because she enjoys her pursuit. A musician may have natural rhythm, but natural talent blossoms from a love for what you do, and, again, that is more likely if you already have some natural talent. Circular.

To find your gifts, think back on what others have praised you for. Look for activities you have enjoyed or done exceptionally well. Seek out a pursuit where you lose track of time. Sometimes, these are found in odd places. If your artwork is amazing, you probably already know it, but may not realize how good you are at visiting with people, sharing ideas, or caring for pets, houses, gardens, or the like. Is your natural talent cleaning? Do you get lost in it, find joy in it, and produce quality work? Then that may be your natural talent—and one that is a needed service. Consider these character archetypes. What describes you the most?

Builder: These people love tools and creating works, whether the tool is a wood carving knife or a computer program. From restoring old Harley Davidson Knuckleheads like my uncle does to building bridges we all drive over, builders do not just see a building—they are entranced by architecture. Often invisible, these people leave their mark on the world in ways we benefit from daily. They are the ones who construct the cathedrals of this world.

Artist: This type loves words, shapes, and colors—from abstract to hyperrealism. While artists also live through payment, they truly live from those who gaze at their paintings, weep or dance upon hearing their music, or hearing someone recite something they wrote—that is a writer's dream! We are seduced when quoted—not from narcissism, but from the joy of being seen when hidden. Could that be a part of love? Artists are those who paint the cathedral walls we gaze upon as our faces are painted by the stained glass windows the builders installed. We read their words and are filled with the spirit of god. We hear their music and cannot help but sing praise to the giver of the muse.

Seeker: Only seekers are finders, but this type seeks wisdom worthy of a sage speaking profound truths in an hour of need. It is not entertainment meant only for distraction. Does our wisdom build up, tear down, or merely divert us from life's purpose? Seekers listen to the divine more so than soothsayers. They long for the greatest wisdom, be it from humankind or wildlife, dreams or fears, Elders or the youngest of children. To a seeker, the value of a book that teaches them cannot be measured—it is invaluable. They fill the pews with bated breath yearning for enlightenment.

Leader: A true leader takes command, not for vainglory, but to lead others to their own greatness. These do not beguile the masses but serve as righteous kings or queens, ruling with a careful balance of mercy and justice. Leaders speak to the congregation and plan for events, whether merriment or mourning. A leader holds a crying child to show all it is okay. They are the ones who whisper in your ear, "You've got this. I have faith in you."

Helper: No leader—indeed no person—can move forward without helpers. Without them, the building would overflow with trash and dirty dishes, the floors would never be clean, and nothing would be in order. From transcribing one day to dusting the tops of paintings the next, helpers set the stage. They may not play the music, but they ensure it can be played and heard. In the back of the audience and behind the stage, the workers draw the curtains of life.

Sentinels: From those who ensure women and children are safe from perverts masquerading as eccentric or nice, to those standing guard as military, police, and security personnel, sentinels are protectors. What an interesting word, that of "security." A sentinel makes sure his wife feels safe or her husband feels respected. True sentinels easily forgo the party, dance, or drinks to make sure everyone gets there, enjoys themselves, and returns home safely. He stands at the door of the cathedral, ever ready to do his job, yet secretly hoping he never has to—that his mere presence would be enough, as it so often is. From firefighters to Marines, the warriors of this world are invaluable.

Healer: From those who pray to those who listen, a true healer seeks to nurture the body, mind, and soul—not just the body! And not just to heal but to prevent future harm. They don't give drugs to mask symptoms and create new problems. Healers have no fear of saying that you are suffering mentally rather than hiding behind the cowardice of accepting you for who you are. To them, a confused mind and bitter soul are no different than a protruding, cancerous tumor. True healers are not always sought. Like an angel or Valkyrie, those who nurse our wounds can be terrifying, but their presence is vital.

Entrepreneur: This archetype is so misunderstood. The businessperson is not just a creator of products people need or enjoy, but also a provider of jobs enabling others to afford clothing, food, housing, travel, and more. One who loves playing with numbers or collecting valuables, be it gold or paper—this is the one who funded the building of the cathedral, the art therein, the wages for sages, and even other people's tithes ultimately came from these.

From host to jester, from instructor to inspirer, every archetype has its shadow. Money can corrupt just as praise and cheer for a finished song also can—how oft does what was for service or god become for us? Ask any preacher who has fallen. And this congregation could be your dance class, a bakery, an elementary school, or indeed a humble church.

In each of these, we can choose to be a hero or a villain. Sadly, many choose villainy or mediocrity over heroism. In modern culture, villainy is less frowned upon than becoming heroic—the idea of heroism is oft met with mockery or dismissed as naïve. Do not reject light in fear of shadows.

Find your archetype, choose your path therein, and refine it—not just through hard work, but smart work, as well as the guidance of mentors.

2. Obsession

Once you find something, start chasing it with a spirit of madness. Even if it turns out to not be the right thing, starting with something will help propel you to your true passion. Only those who are obsessed with victory will have victory. To achieve wealth, you must fully devote yourself to your natural talent.

To become a great writer, writing (and reading for its purpose) must take up more time every day than all other activities combined, including sleep. Obsession is not writing for an hour and then playing games. You have to learn ways to make meals a little faster, or not spend as long in the shower just to stand in the hot water—and even then, you are dreaming about your pursuit. There are 24 hours in a day, if one writer can work and still find five hours to read and write, then you should aim for eight, and then 16 on days off. Allow yourself to be obsessed, or accept failure.

Yet, if obsessed, you do not leave this to chance. You set obtainable but fully challenging goals. Do not just study and work, study the finest material and work as smart as you can. Do not merely study and work hard, or you will have no clear goal, otherwise you'll have no finish line or way of knowing when you've failed. And how can you shift your aim if there is no target to miss?

To do this, to give yourself to the spirit of obsession—and be devoted to your heroic self—write at the top of the next page the most ambitious goal you want made manifest within four years—whatever you wish to pursue with absolute obsession.

Under this, write a list of two-year goals that will lead you to the four-year milestone. Repeat this process for one year, six months, one month, one week, and finally for today, broken into time slots of morning, afternoon, and evening.

Once you do this, type or write it out. Adjust your methods as needed. The six-months, one-month, and one-week trajectories will shift often, but it is achievable daily goals—written down each night or morning—that will propel you forward and bring your talent to the light it deserves.

My Magnificent Obsession:

2 Years:

1 Year:

6 Months:

1 Month:

This Morning:

This Afternoon:

This Evening:

3. A Tutor

A great tutor can magnify your passions and refine your skills many times over. The best tutor of all? None other than yourself. Who is reading this workbook, after all?

This does not mean going to night school or only watching free content online. Find sites that offer classes on banking, gardening, woodworking, photography, cooking, and the like. Whatever your passion is, find classes and learn from them. By doing so, you will become your best mentor, and your skills will improve.

Looking at the passion of poetry, vegetable gardening, and making wooden bowls, could you also do side work in writing songs, growing flowers, or making old-fashioned pipes? What you learn from making Oom Paul pipes could easily make you twice as skilled at bowl-making. Learning how to write songs will enhance your poems, and growing flowers will teach you hidden tricks for growing vegetables— plus, the extra bees will help your crop!

To have wealth, you must pursue your passion, or at least *a* passion. The wrong one is a million times better than none at all. Considering this, write 10 things you will do to further your education. Painters always improve when learning how to use other mediums, such as charcoal, hyper-realistic pen and ink, and oil paint—always! How will enhancing your education be done? Books? Online classes? Finding a mentor instead of talking about it?

Write this on the next page. Then pick one and learn from this one thing as deeply as possible. Once you have absorbed all that is useful, pick another one and grow.

My education will be enhanced by these tutors:

1.

2.

3.

4.

5.

6.

7.

8.

9.

10.

> *"Our life is frittered away by detail.*
> *Simplicity, simplicity, simplicity!*
> *I say, let our affairs be as two or three, and not a*
> *hundred or a thousand. Simplify, simplify!"*
> *-Henry David Thoreau*

Without clear achievable milestones, we sacrifice ideals for temporary luxuries and distractions. This creates, not an unshaped void, but a vacuum that cannot be filled with the garbage we are told we want.

Invest in yourself and take action. Do this, and your path, or at least the next step, will illuminate itself.

If your life's passion is to own a raspberry farm, but you are sleeping on the couch at your parents' house, you can still take steps—baby steps. I know that may sound like a unique situation and not applicable to your life, but consider how this can indeed apply to you: Find a job or internship at a farm, even if it is not for raspberries. Then, also find a gardener who has raspberries, and someone who sells basil to local restaurants. Learn from these people. Even if you don't have five cents to your name, look at farmland. No, not for a vision board or to mentally will it into your life, but to see the price, the soil conditions, the weather conditions, and the like. Even if you have no money to invest, still invest in yourself by going to the library and reading books on farming, such as how to start a farm, pruning, and everything there is to know about raspberries, from pest controls to profit margins.

But I remind you of the simple: we all grow. You may one day take a greater interest in blueberries, viticulture, or even barn building. One door may close, but many others open. So allow yourself the greatest dream of all children: the ability to grow.

> *"The Seven Social Sins are:*
> *Wealth without work.*
> *Pleasure without conscience.*
> *Knowledge without character.*
> *Commerce without morality.*
> *Science without humanity.*
> *Worship without sacrifice.*
> *Politics without principle."*
> *-Frederick Lewis Donaldson*

Is this real?

Let's say you know someone who loves playing the flute. That is her natural talent. She gets lost in it. So she decides to give herself to it and begins to practice many hours a day.

She would become even better, right?

Now, what if she went online and took different classes, not just on flute music, but piano and drum, how to play music with others, different styles, and even how to write her own music? She does this, not just for a weekend, but for the next four years.

How much better would she be than before? Three times? Ten? Twelve?

Due to this, she starts to make a good living through music. She can quit her job and put in fifty hours more every week to her craft. She can afford a top-of-the-line flute, play music with other highly talented artists, take high-end private classes, and produce studio-quality recordings. Now, tens of thousands of people have the joy of hearing her music!— while dancing with a loved one, while making dinner for grandmother, while dreaming up their own art, or while walking past a restaurant where her songs are playing, drawn in by the music as much as the aroma of food and smiles on people's faces. We benefit more from her music than she does from charging an average price for above-average music.

How would you define her progress?

"There's no scarcity of opportunity to make
a living at what you love; there is only a
scarcity of resolve to make it happen."
-Dr. Wayne W. Dyer

But now for the bad part: What if despite all that beauty, she thought publishing her music was selling out? What if she never tried at all? (Or just thought she was trying). What if you had no idea this woman could play the flute to begin with? What if that person were you?

Even if you are homeless, buying a flute and some beginner books at used shops is not impossible—even if you are like me and refuse to beg. You could work for a shop in exchange for these items, and then play and play until you are good enough to make a fair wage on a street corner. You can do this whether you are starting in the middle of the race or 10 miles before the starting line. Doesn't matter. The race is only with yourself. There is no competition with all the other musicians—only with yourself. And never forget: The starting line is also the finish line. It is a place where everyone cheers, not just at the finish but at the start. And the diehard fans, the ones who matter most, cheer at every hurdle, every lap, and perhaps the loudest of all when you fall down, but rise again.

"He who every morning plans the transactions of that day and follows that plan carries a thread that will guide him through the labyrinth of the most busy life."
-Victor Hugo

I grant you, that someone who loves to write poetry faces pretty rough odds of making a living at it, but he has more wealth than if he gave up poems for only corporate work.

But now for me to hit you where it hurts:

You're likely not any good at what you are passionate about for the following reasons:

1. You already think you're good, and this means you stay where you are. How much have you explored outside of your comfort zone? How much challenge have you endured?

2. If you are not better this year than last, your passion is a hobby. And while you should keep your hobby, you should also keep your job and focus more on your job than you are.

Never stay only in education, not even for a day—take action toward your passion, for success cannot occur without stumbling and failing as you strive to move forward.

"Making money isn't hard in itself.
What's hard is to earn it doing something
worth devoting one's life to."
-Carlos Ruiz Zafón

However, if you still do not know what you want, then you either already have it or you don't know who you are. For most, it is a mixture of both. To dig into this, play with dreams versus distractions:

A dream: To be healthy and fit.

A distraction: Watching TV and eating cookies.

A dream: Finding a loving partner.

A distraction: Lust that poorly imitates intimacy.

Who do you *really* want to be?

Ask your family what you enjoyed as a child. Spend time alone in nature and be silent. Reflect on what had caught your attention more than once. Have you always enjoyed looking at stones? Do paintings catch your eye? Is it sharing meals or cleaning homes? Music or battle? Even if you come to the wrong thing, the wrong thing is better than no-thing! Often, those who pursue music discover they are dancers. Those who dream of painting become woodcarvers, photographers, or, of course, painters.

Your passion may hide in the word "community," which could lead you to care for Elders, become a death doula, or gather your family or town closer together in festival. I once knew a woman who loved art but did not have a steady hand—so she hosted art parties and sponsored artists. She found a way to paint through others. Find something, whether it's cleaning rivers or caring for abandoned pets—we will all be blessed when you find your joy.

Everything in your life is there because you put it there—well over 99% of it at least is! What do you have in your house—are you being forced by anyone to have it there? Likely not. Your job—does anyone kidnap you each morning or did you choose to work there? From faith to diet, from job to hobbies, even friends and family you see, you have chosen them all. You don't have to choose the same or differently! Instead, see who you have been and who you want to be, and be honest with yourself in answering: Who, precisely, am I becoming? What is my actual trajectory?

> *"Time is the most valuable coin in your life.*
> *You and you alone will determine how that coin*
> *will be spent. Be careful that you do not let*
> *other people spend it for you."*
> *-Carl Sandburg*

What in your life, if sacrificed (removed), would increase your ability to pursue your passion? If you have children, they should be your passion, but have you spoiled or neglected them to the point where they've become burdens instead? Or have you neglected your own pursuits? That harms your children's well-being, as much as it does yours. All of my family is glad my mom pursued the piano, cello, trumpet, and fiddle—none of us felt she should have spent more time at work, gardening, or with us kids. After all, if she had abandoned her music, she would no longer be herself.

From aspiring poets to bodybuilders, there is a need for dedicated periods of time where all you do is write or train—not write and surf the internet, not exercise and take pictures for social media. This allows you to pursue who you are, rather than dabble.

Be obsessed! Many sacrifice who they are for their job, for their family, or to fit in, but we love you because you are you. If you stop dancing, who are you? If a man who loves to train gives that up so he can spend more time with his kids, well, maybe that sounds noble, but just who is spending time with the kids? A sacrificial goat? Maybe the kids would be better off with a man. Should a mother give up dancing, poetry, or rock climbing to get in an extra hour to do the dishes? I think her husband would be better off with a wife than a maid. A clean house is nice, and a man ought to spend ample time with his children, but if both parents block off time to enhance who they are by consolidating unimportant things—then family time will be enriched through time management and you will be a hero to all you love.

What you care about + what you are drawn to + what you have some natural talent in + something you lose track of time while doing + allowing yourself to become obsessed out of joy = your passion. Add to that mentorship, and it becomes beautiful. It becomes you.

Algorithms For Finding Work

Look at your life today and how you got here. You "got a job, moved, and met someone" is not an answer to this question. How and why did you get this job? Why not a better one? Did you work on yourself and your skills to increase the pay? Do you even have a job?

Presently, I work at multiple vineyards. The locations are stunning, with peaceful fields and gardens. People often come up and ask me to take their pictures. I hear joyous laughter and get to visit with people from all over the world. It is wonderful. Yet, so few people apply for these jobs. Some years, no one applies at all—even though every week I hear people say how much they would love to work where I work.

I also volunteer at two locations where I care for injured and orphaned wildlife. Everyone swoons at the pictures and then goes on and on about how much they would love to do that, yet they never show up. Do they have time? Yes. Many of them are unemployed or have weekends with nothing to do but watch TV—they choose to have nothing else to do!

"The bad news is time flies.
The good news is you're the pilot."
-Michael Altshul

Look for algorithms that have worked for you. Some patterns of behavior help a lot of people, so they gain a cult-like following (journaling is a big one), while other methods are seldom heard about.

Have you ever picked up stones and felt as dejected as her?
Yet, difficult work leads to a field filled with food.
A home filled with laughter.
Eyes that always look as if seeing a smiling child.
Even on the days when our work is picking up stones.

The best algorithm I learned came when I was young. When heading into town to look for a job, I stopped and saw my dad first. He asked me what kind of job I was going to get, and I said I was going to apply everywhere that was hiring and see what I could find. He said, quite loudly and with disgust, "That's stupid!" When I asked why, he said, "What do you want to do?"

Being young and somewhat foolish, I answered honestly and said I didn't want to work. I wanted to have time to go to fairs and hang out with friends. He thought about it earnestly, then said, "You should go get a job at Spears. They work four days a week, so you could have three-day weekends." Again, I resisted and wrote it off by saying they weren't hiring. He said, "Who cares! Go in any way. If they won't hire you, tell them you'll work for free for two weeks. When they see how good you are, they will hire you." I did, and they hired me. And for many years, I enjoyed having free time along with decent work and pay.

"When we combine the idea of prosperity with an intention
for our highest good and the highest
good of all life, we create true wealth."
-Amy Leigh Mercree

That method, that algorithm of choosing where I wanted to work, stayed with me. Later, I wanted to work at a wildlife sanctuary, but knew you needed degrees, and surely people were waiting in line to work there. But I went in and asked anyway. It turned out they desperately needed help, but only with the "barnyard animals," as they called them. A job no one wanted. But I grew up on a farm, and within a few days, they saw that I did my job well and enjoyed working with any animal, and soon I was also working with the wildlife there. Turned out that it was a test. Most people who come in only wanted to work with the wildlife and so quit after a day of shoveling manure and stacking hay bales. Very similar to life.

I have taught women's self-defense for decades, but it took many years to earn my black belts, and even more years of instructing before I was good enough to host shorter classes that could improve people's lives. But I kept at it regardless of the time investment.

I also write (surprise, surprise), and that, too, took time before I was any good.

The point? I get to choose where I work. So do you. Even if it takes time and effort, you can have jobs you enjoy. I sometimes tell my friends that at work today I had to taste-test wines and chocolate to see which paired better, as that is part of the job, or I show them a scenic picture and say, "This is my office," and they swoon. But part of my job is also working on smelly water pumps, getting pricked by roses, dealing with mosquitoes, and working some days in 100-degree heat. Every job has difficult portions. The number of times an animal has urinated on me, or worse, died in my hands, I cannot count. But I love caring for gardens and the wildlife that lives in them.

For you, it may be cleaning or making fine meals. Imagine if, for a living, you made cakes all day and had people come by for the best coffee they've ever had. Every day, you'd hear laughter, see smiles, and receive cards in the mail thanking you for your hard work. It would be wonderful. But you would also get a burn or two, have to be careful and fight the temptation of eating too many goodies, and sometimes deal with customers who were anything but pleasant. Seek not perfection, but joy and worth instead.

Seeking the work I want to do is an algorithm I cherish, but, like everyone else in the world, I have algorithms that harm me as well, from anger when interrupted to being drawn to alcohol and depression. I have my battles, same as you.

"It has long been an axiom of mine that the little things are infinitely the most important."
-Sir Arthur Conan Doyle

Money enhances who you are, including your troubles. If you are a scoundrel, money will enhance that. If you are a loving and giving person, money will amplify your generosity. If you spend so much that you go into debt, more money will not stop that. If you want the most from this workbook, couple it with the rest of the *Hero* series, otherwise, your troubles may only grow. One who is in debt when making $2,000 a month will go deeper in debt when making $10,000 a month. One who saves money at $2,000 a month will become wealthy when making $10,000 a month.

The biggest and simplest rule of wealth must never be ignored: Live below your means. If that sounds difficult, then increase your means—but start now by living below your means, even if that entails eating lentils and rice while picking dandelions out of your yard for greens—or even living with other family. You can do live below your income. You *must*! Otherwise, you'll not have financial freedom.

Think about it. Someone who makes 10 times more than you—do they work 10 times as many hours? Not unless they figured out how to have more than 24 hours a day!

Say you are a janitor who cleans four houses. If you clean eight, you'll double your income. Now let's say you only clean three, but they are businesses or clients who need someone like you: trustworthy (can you be trusted to clean a bank or an office working on new tech to patent), reliable (you show up on time and get the job done even if it takes work off the clock), and not only competent but truly passionate and committed (when you leave and see a can in the parking lot, you pick it up and recycle it instead of leaving it for the next guy). Or are you looking for above-average pay while being content with staying a below-average person? Doesn't work that way. Being above average is not about appearances or diplomas, it's about grit and actions. People often ask if I went to school to become a viticulturist, and I answer, "No. I went to work. And now, schools come to me."

"We need the best plumbers. We need the best contractors. We need the best carpenters. We need the best lecturers. There has to be a hierarchy of quality. Not only so that we know who the best are and can reward them properly, but so that we can reward them so they keep being the best. If you have a great educator, if you have a great leader, if you have a great thinker, you want to reward them so they keep thinking and they keep educating. So they can tell you something. It's not a reward for their intrinsic being. It's a calculated move on your part, to suck everything out of them that's valuable as fast as you can. That's what a hierarchy of competence is for."
-Dr. Jordan Peterson

If you want to improve, invest in yourself like you matter. You do! Now, you might be tempted to think you don't, but you are awesome because you can improve and are improving. For me, it was a harsh realization one day while driving to work, and though you may not agree with this, it woke me up when I said aloud: "I would like a girlfriend, but I would not want to be with a woman who would accept someone like me as a partner. I want someone who wants a better man than me!" That meant I had to become a better man. I had to improve.

And I have.

And still can.

Years ago (when I first began writing this series), I was homeless (thankfully, I had a car to live in), had no bank account, wallet, or job, and was curled up and shivering as the snow blew so hard it often froze my car doors shut. I thought of killing myself every day and wept every night. All I wanted to do was drink, and I drank alone because I had no friends. None. Now? I have friends, smile, enjoy my work, and so much more. I may not have amazing riches—but I am no longer hungry or cold! I still battle emotional difficulties, but they are no longer making my life worse, and I actually have more good moments than bad ones.

> *"They say a person needs just three things*
> *to be truly happy in this world:*
> *someone to love,*
> *something to do,*
> *and something to hope for."*
> *-Tom Bodett*

First, I did everything I could to work on my situations and emotions (and here is the key part) for that time. The fact that I was moving forward at all was nothing shy of a miracle and a victory. From going to therapy to taking Ashwagandha, I read books and recited mantras as often as I could, and slowly found work that was not what I wanted, but needed, which was simple. It took a long time to let go of the poverty mindset, which in itself has nothing to do with being broke, just being broken.

But enough about me.

Now let's move on to step one of increasing income. Everything up to this point was just groundwork. Let's get started on building.

"Do not wait: the time will never be 'just right.' Start where you stand, and work whatever tools you may have at your command and better tools will be found as you go along."
-Napoleon Hill

Starting

An author once told me to write, even if I didn't know what to say, and even if what I wrote was rubbish. "If you write 5,000 words and have to delete it, you are still better off than if you had not written at all. You have grown. You know what not to do. And each day you do this, you will get better."

You have to start.

I started putting my writings online, but only after (embarrassing to say) more than a year of studying how to do it. I was stumbling around like a person who had never seen the Internet before. It was awful. Building a website was costly and difficult, and I was getting no traffic—my goodness this was difficult!

What I should have done, and what I do now, is what I am telling you to do: just start. Read, but take action. And the first place to start? Begin saving money.

Whether you are rich, homeless, or middle class, it doesn't matter—start setting aside money. You may have to find a way to open a bank account, or you may have to stop investing so you can save more each month for larger goals. But to do this, you must audit yourself. It is what our government should do to itself, for sure, and it is what we see in others so easily. "If Sally would stop buying those expensive cosmetics, she could afford schooling." Well, what about all the times you eat out? Or the three (or more) hours every day you waste watching TV or playing video games? What could you become or earn with 20-plus hours each week of working toward your dreams, rather than watching the dreams of others?

This is not to say you cannot enjoy life or take a break, but do we need so much downtime when we are feeling so down? Let's build ourselves up! And to do so, even if it is so small you think it would never amount to anything, start saving today. Live below your income, even if that means cleaning a convenience store in exchange for food, like a homeless couple I met recently. What honorable people!

Start! Even if it means working! Even if you do not know where you are going yet!

"Love in your heart
is better than gold in your hands."
-Matshona Dhliwayo

Let's say, in three years, you decide you want to open a studio for both yoga and powerlifting. Awesome! You found a dream! Perhaps a husband likes powerlifting, and the wife loves yoga—or the other way around, as, hey, I've seen that, too. Regardless, you decide to build your dream. If, for the last three years, you have been saving back money, you may have enough for a yearlong lease, insurance, and to fully stock the yoga side. You might only have just enough for stones on the powerlifting side, but—here is the greatest lesson in this workbook—you decide to **start**.

If you do not start, then what good would it be if you knew everything there is to know about yoga, powerlifting, owning a gym, marketing, and so forth? There would be no studio to open!

It may take a year to find a good location or decide where you want to live, but start looking, and work on learning what you need in that location. And this applies to everything, even if your dream is to make jam. How far do you want this business to grow? Do you want to see your jams in stores locally or nationwide? Then, plan for this growth, but start in your kitchen today, not tomorrow. Every food product has started in someone's kitchen. You are no different. And yes, most gyms start in a garage, but you can grow it over 10 years to have a dozen locations, learning how to market along the way.

Start.

Want to babysit? Start by learning all the laws and safety measures for the children and yourself. Go speak with other babysitters by offering to buy them a fancy meal in exchange for their advice. Enjoy chit-chatting during the meal and set a half-hour afterward for their advice. Learn from books, yes, but also give yourself a time limit. "I am going to advertise my services and start asking for work in exactly three months. There it is, in red, on my calendar—I better make some calls right now!"

Start!

There are reasons why you can't. Of course!

There are also reasons why you can. Of course!

Which one is worth your time?

Lack of pure focus is multiplied by unrefined and doubted dreams.

> *"If you can't do great things,*
> *do small things in a great way."*
> *-Napoleon Hill*

You need a heaven to run toward and a hell to run away from. Without a hell to run away from, well, you will just aimlessly meander toward someone else's idea of heaven. And worse, if you only have a hell to run from and no heaven to run towards, then why run at all? What would you run towards? You're just in hell, and you're done. Anxiety in front will block the door, but if it is behind you it will push you through the door—thus, you must define what that door is. The more clearly you know what is heaven (and I do not mean the pearly gates) and what is hell (no pitchforks and lakes of fire, although sometimes it feels that way) the more likely you will find a meaningful path.

"The longer I live, the more I read, the more patiently I think, and the more anxiously I inquire, the less I seem to know. Do justly. Love mercy. Walk humbly. This is enough."
-John Adams

What is the heaven you want to run towards:

What is the hell you want to run away from:

"The secret to getting ahead is getting started."
-Mark Twain

In order, name what needs to be done to start pursuing your heaven and fleeing from your hell. Beside each, add a brief explanation of how you will do it.

1.

2.

3.

4.

5.

6.

7.

8.

9.

10.

Take the steps you can, even if it doesn't complete everything. Starting and consistency, despite failures, are the greatest ways to increase income and wealth.

You are not doing this to become a hero.
You are a hero because you are moving forward.

Adventuring forth will cause you to grow as a person and learn that victory requires failures. Messing up isn't really messing up—it's part of the journey, so enjoy it. Yet, having special skills helps, so let's hasten victory with three of the most important tactics there are; investigating the landscape, removing the negatives, and doubling the positives.

"In the midst of chaos,
there is also opportunity."
-Sun Tzu

Investigating The Landscape

Visit similar businesses before and after beginning yours. Say you want to start a coffee shop. Your first step should be visiting one to three new coffee shops every day. Check on those nearby as well as the highest-rated ones that are states away. While visiting, ask things like:

"What is your best-selling coffee or treat?"

"Do you roast your beans?"

"What kind of beans are they?—I'd love to buy a bag from you."

"How do you market this place? I'm not trying to pitch myself as a marketer. I'm just curious."

Regardless of the business you are pursuing, ask about their marketing strategies, how they attract customers, and their best sellers. Look for any unconventional tactics as well. In the case of the coffee shop, take notes about the store—not just from their answers but also from your observations. Ask yourself: What music is playing? Is it too loud? Are the restrooms easy to find? Where is the service top-notch and where is it lacking? What about the location makes or breaks this place? Write out details and more questions while you sit and enjoy your *small* coffee (I mean, you are visiting several coffee shops today, so small is best).

> *"What if the only thing standing in the way of your greatness was that you just had to go after everything obsessively, persistently, and as though your life depended on it?"*
> *-Grant Cardone*

Next, test what you gathered. Let's say you bought coffee from 24 places that stood out to you among 280 shops. Brew them up, weighing the grams of grounds and measuring the ounces of water so they are the same, and taste-test them over and over until you narrow them down to five. Revisit those places (as well as a few other shops that had the best service or vibes) as often as you can, and enjoy a coffee while writing and refining your business model.

After six months, you'll know where to buy the best fair-trade Arabic Coffee in bulk and what roasting equipment to invest in—you'll have visually measured the areas and determined the best amount of space needed. During this process, ask more questions, from schooling to insurance, to even how to hire the best staff. Become friends with the owner and ask, "If you could do it all over, what would you do differently? What mistakes did you make along the way?"

Continue to research, not your competitors, but like-minded people, to learn about new trends and old tricks. Find joy in sitting there and asking yourself endless questions, such as, "Are these chairs comfortable?" or, "Is the location of the bathroom private or will it make the shop stink?" When you see a regular, ask, "What is your favorite thing about this place?" She may tell you there are chargers and outlets at each table, that it feels more like a home than a store, or even how she loves all the birdfeeders outside the windows. Learn from all, and your company will shine. Your guests will also reap the rewards.

"You wasted $150,000 on an education you could have got for $1.50 in late fees at the public library."
-Matt Damon, Good Will Hunting

Cutting Out What Doesn't Work

As you progress, find ways to cut steps, no matter how small or large. At work, can you pick up three items instead of two? How much time does that save, and how many more units can you produce this way? What if that tool you need was closer, or could you use something easier?

"Remember that your real wealth can be measured not by what you have, but by what you are."
-Napoleon Hill

In a big kitchen, it may be impossible to have everything within reach, but what if all the things you use the most were? If you use two knives, toasted sesame seed oil, and garlic for nearly every meal, and you always use them at the stove, could you place a shelf there for those items?—oh, and salt, pepper, and cumin could go on that, too!

Every job can be made a little more streamlined. At the job I mentioned earlier (Spears), I replaced the full-time welder, the full-time material cutter, as well as the half-day shipping employee. How? I started as the welder, but I rearranged some palates so all my parts were closer, changed the restocking schedule so I would never run out of supplies, and communicated with everyone to ensure I prioritized items needed most and what would fit on their shelves. Soon, I was not only caught up but had extra time so they gave me another job. I did the same thing there, optimizing cutting patterns and focusing on high-demand items. Not only did I save the company more money than I made, but I cut down production time there as well by figuring out how many layers I could cut while keeping good measurements. Soon, what was a full-time job was now less than a half-time job, so they put me in shipping—and that was a mess! Until I removed wasted motions.

We can do this at work, as well as at home. If we are going to use the garden hose right there again tomorrow, then is rolling it up important? Or is there a way to roll it up so it is not tangled the next day? Are we stopping at an alleged convenience store every morning and fighting traffic when we could buy what we need in bulk, thereby giving ourselves 15 more minutes every day to start and work on our projects?

Martial artists seek to eliminate all wasted motion. When people start, removing wasted motions is one of the bigger tasks of the instructor. When an untrained person jumps, for example, she will bring her feet in a little, bend down slightly, drop her hands, then partially commit to the jump so the front leg comes up and the back leg is barely off the floor. Then she kicks once the back foot is on the floor, lands too far forward, and so scoots back to reposition everything in her stance. This, all of it, is wasted motion. She must work diligently to remove all tells until she can jump straight up, kick while the back leg is tucked, and land in the same spot in a perfect stance. It seems simple but takes many months for a natural (years for most people) to learn.

"Don't let mental blocks control you.
Set yourself free.
Confront your fear
and turn the mental blocks
into building blocks."
-Dr. Roopleen

Cutting wasted motion can be seen in many places. Watch a pro chef slicing a carrot. They have honed their skills and can go so fast, and the slices are the same size—if I tried that, I might not even have fingers left! They are done with a bundle; meanwhile, I am still working on one carrot!

Or look at someone who takes care of linens. Some, even though this is their job, are not that impressive, but others have clever methods for folding clothes. It might look like OCD (obsessive-compulsive disorder) and like it took weeks to do, but it is not; it is quality work. And you do not get quality work with sloppy effort and pointless steps.

Try this today: Find three simple things where you can cut wasted steps. And I mean simple. Could you place the hairbrush in a better location, so it is easier? Are you waiting to brush your hair because someone else is in the restroom? Or maybe they are always waiting for you? Or perhaps the brush doesn't have a home, so you are always looking for it? Do this with three things, and aim for simplicity.

Three small-sized changes you made and the result:

1.

2.

3.

"Simple, genuine goodness is the best capital to found the business of this life upon. It lasts when fame and money fail, and is the only riches we can take out of this world with us."
-Louisa May Alcott

Now try this exercise with three medium-sized things to remove wasted motions from. Even if it takes more work than it saves initially, see what you can do.

Three medium-sized changes to try this week:

1.

2.

3.

More work than it saves? Let's say you spend 12 hours organizing your shop so it is nicer and tools are where you need them. And while it will likely save more time than this, let's say you know it only saved you 15 minutes a week. Not a huge difference? When working in a flow state, those 15 uninterrupted minutes may lead to higher quality work or give you the chance to perfect your craft. And, of course, you may just spend it looking out of a window watching birds at the feeder instead—that is okay, too. Life isn't all about accomplishments, and enjoying those birds may do more for you than a little extra income, to be honest. The point here is to create a more peaceful workspace, while honing a critical business skill. This is powerful. Before reading on, take some time to start implementing these improvements now.

What if life was twice as complex as it is now? What about 10 times as complex? Would you be able to get anything done, or would you just sink into the abyss? Now, what if it was half or even a tenth as complex—what would that feel like?

Some complexity is essential, of course, but removing a hundred distractions will improve your life beyond what you can even dream. That stack of unread books, the box of things to sell, the curtain that is torn and not hanging right—these are not trivial things!

"Have regular hours for work and play; make each day both useful and pleasant, and prove that you understand the worth of time by employing it well. Then youth will bring few regrets, and life will become a beautiful success."
-Louisa May Alcott

Is there junk mail you can cancel? A cluttered desk to tidy? A stack of old CDs to go through or a kitchen cupboard overflowing with unused pans? The reduction in chaotic complexity is not a measurement of one thing corrected, but an accumulation of hundreds. No longer having to walk around that box and only having clothes you like that fit—these things add up and free the creative mind so wealth can come into your life. This is the method of subtracting to add and adding to subtract.

What if you could only subtract, be it in business or relationships, to improve your wealth? What if cutting out TV and junk food would help your marriage? Actually, that isn't a what-if question because you already know it would improve your time together. What if you cut out those 20 customers who cause 95% of your problems? If the worst drama-causing employee were gone, would happiness increase?

This is the 80/20 rule in action, though sometimes it is 90/10 or 70/30. But it is still often the case that 80% of your income or joy comes from 20% of your efforts, and 90% of stress might come from 10% of your customers or family.

If you work in the advertising industry, for instance what would happen if you chose to represent only the 10 companies you respect most, rather than the twenty you don't? Would that improve your happiness? For me, I sleep soundly knowing I do not promote garbage.

"Libraries will get you through times of no money better than money will get you through times of no libraries."
-Anne Herbert

The list of what to cut from your routine to enhance life is frighteningly long. So, pick only a few things to start; once done, revisit this question: How can I use subtraction to add? What is your:

* Top stressor:
Top waste of money:
Biggest waste of time:
Most harmful habit to your health:
Quality that makes you the least trustworthy:

* Do not cut out family. If your wife or husband is your biggest stressor, devote 10 times the effort you think it requires to work through that difficulty and make it right. To avoid the pain of divorce, you may need to spend twice as much time with her, start baking together, or learn to manage your financial difficulties. Address smaller problems now before they grow into huge monsters that affect not only your relationship but your whole community. You are both worth the effort.

These steps are so critical that without them, success in any pursuit—love, passion, or craft—is unattainable. Removing wasted motions will help you more than most books on romance and business combined. It is that powerful. Do not skip it. Apply these lessons again and again, even when it seems like you cannot think of another thing to reduce or remove. Do so, and you will succeed in wealth.

"Top 15 things money can't buy:
Time.
Happiness.
Inner Peace.
Integrity.
Love.
Character.
Manners.
Health.
Respect.
Morals.
Trust.
Patience.
Class.
Common sense.
Dignity."
-Roy T. Bennett

Note: *Every one of those is wrong. If you don't believe me, consider the wealth of a book.*

Doubling Down

With the free time gained by removing pointless steps, one can do something that sounds basic: doubling your education. Imagine how much compound interest, not just in wealth, but in talent and enjoyment that would produce. If you know your beloved is tickled pink when you tell a pun, write a poem, or even build something in the home, then why not double down on that, too? But how can you, unless you also cut out what doesn't work (wasted motion)?

"If people knew how hard I had to work to gain my mastery,
it would not seem so wonderful at all."
-Michelangelo Buonarroti

How many times have you seen husbands tell jokes that clearly their partners do not like? By cutting out the twenty bad jokes that upset her, there is more time to compliment her cooking, which she does like. And if her cooking is horrid? Complaining won't help, but giving her gifts, such as a big wooden spoon with a wood-burning of her favorite animal on it, great cookbooks, and lovingly making meals with her is what builds love, as well as great meals. Or say she's annoyed that he wasted time and money on a project, yet complains he isn't manly if he hires it out. What if you cut that out, and double down on what makes him so proud to have you in his life? What if that was making him a goodie and eating with him in the garage and telling him he is cute when he is all greasy?—but that he better shower if he wants a hug later! Those things—those little powerful moments—are what can turn a dull relationship into a thing of beauty. And business is no different, even if your healthy pursuit of wealth is growing basil for local restaurants.

Doubling what works, and removing what does not, doesn't always produce results the first time, as we are doing so little that double is unnoticeable. Take, for example, a wife who cooks a nice meal once every 10 years. If she doubled her effort, her husband would not notice. Or if he brings her flowers once every decade, would she notice if it changed to once every five years? Granted, there comes a time when it is over the top. Flowers one to four times a month will likely produce better results than every half hour or every decade. But the man will have to up it and up it again before he finds where there starts to be a drop in appreciation and admiration.

"In dwelling, live close to the ground.
In thinking, keep to the simple.
In conflict, be fair and generous.
In governing, don't try to control.
In work, do what you enjoy.
In family life, be completely present."
-Lao Tzu

But let's back up a moment. Say a man worked on a farm growing basil and made a low wage. He cuts out what does not work by going into business for himself, and not growing a certain kind of basil that's too time-consuming. He then doubles down on the best methods he had learned by working for someone else and removes all wasted motion so the job is easier and more rewarding in a myriad of ways. This is good, but it is not good enough.

Experimentation & Examination

The only way to find new things that work, as simple as this will sound, is to try new things—not too many and not too few. Just enough that it remains enjoyable without distracting from the main focus of cutting wasted motions and doubling down on what is effective.

"The difference between ordinary and extraordinary
is that little extra."
-Jimmy Johnson

Consider the basil farmer (this story could apply to knitting, car sales, romance in a marriage, or exercise, so take a moment to reflect and apply it to what you have started). Let's say he is growing three varieties of basil that sell well and perform consistently. Since he has cut out what doesn't work and has found ways to optimize his greenhouse production, he finds he has room in his third greenhouse and some extra time. So, he tries 15 new varieties of heirloom basil. While 14 of them either produced little, didn't grow, tasted bitter, or didn't appeal to buyers, that one, the lemon basil, just became the best seller!

After a year, he again doubles what works while continuing to remove what doesn't, so his farm expands. He hires other people at a fair wage to work it, teaching them methods to make the work easier, faster, and more enjoyable. He treats these people like what they swiftly become: good friends—good friends with whom he is upfront, making it clear that while he may not want to, he won't hesitate to let them go if they breach his trust, even a little.

Now, with more time, he tries 3 more types of basil, and he also plants test beds. One uses kelp as a fertilizer, another incorporates more sand, as he's read that helps. After experimenting and refining his methods for three years, he finds a great combination and achieves a crop yield that's 15% higher. That may not sound like much, until you realize he now has 45 greenhouses, went into dried herbs and pesto spreads, and that 15% increase is now worth 10 times what he used to make per year. And his family, community, and favorite charity (a children's hospital), are all better off because of him. And who knows? Maybe he derived most of his inspiration while listening to a certain artist's flute. And maybe in three years, he will retire with no more than a first-grade education. But he only succeeded because he started and persisted.

"The human race is a monotonous affair. Most people spend the greatest part of their time working in order to live, and what little freedom remains so fills them with fear that they seek out any and every means to be rid of it."
-Johann Wolfgang von Goethe

Yet, what if he never tried that lemon basil, never started selling pesto, never hired another person to help, or merely kept working at a job he loved but with people who didn't value him? That favorite pasta sauce you buy—do you think that company's story is different?

Some ask their partner how he or she wants to be loved, but what if neither knew how much they enjoyed sweet words, kisses on the ear, or long walks on a beach—cliché or not! Through playful experimenting and then examining the results, you can grow as a person and company in ways you have never considered. So take a moment and write below on how this basil farmer's story could be applied to your life. Let it be a rough draft—you do not need to articulate a clever plan that hindsight would be proud of. You just have to start and persist.

"If you don't write when you don't have time for it,
you won't write when you do have time for it."
-Katerina Stoykova Klemer

Writing

The basil farmer didn't need a formal education, but he still needed education. Few jobs require a traditional degree, and I have seen formal education cripple more people than it has helped. And since education is endless, apply what you learn before learning more. But the greatest way to learn and progress is through writing.

By writing out wisdom and unique skills, and refining them as you move forward, you deeply internalize and create something akin to a personal teacher's manual. This practice prevents forgetting methods of enhancement and allows you to refine steps that might otherwise go unnoticed.

This is profoundly important.

In martial arts, there is a common saying: "An instructor also learns from the students." What we know is amazing, but not as amazing as what we don't know. When you instruct someone in your passion or job, they will ask "Why?" at every step, forcing you to explain it simply so they can follow along. Their repetitive questions force us to look at the tools we use and the steps we take. Are they as effective as the ideas a fresh set of eyes provides? By showing someone how to work a press, you'll realize how many pointless tasks you do, as well as the smart steps you have made. But the student may well point out something you never saw, earning the business more than they're paid.

Writing these insights down and refining them over time is the best way to learn!

Begin by writing one page on your passion. Speak on tricks of your trade, steps you follow, or how you derive inspiration. It doesn't matter if your page is rubbish because it only means there's room to refine it. In doing so you will sharpen your thinking and the actions that stem from it. Get a piece of paper or open a new file, and write one page. Include a list of things to eliminate, a list of what you plan to double down on, and experiments you're interested in trying.

Don't just read that last paragraph. Start writing a little. It only works if you work.

"When he worked, he really worked.
But when he played, he really played."
-Dr. Seuss

Add a little each day and refine it. By doing so, you will refine yourself and gain an edge towards wealth—be it money or health, recipes or the hearth of home. Even if currently homeless, the home (not just house) you will one day have shall reap the rewards of the foundation of wealth you're building through enhancing the foundation of thinking (that of writing).

Inspiration

Many proclaim that if you wait for inspiration, you will never get any work done. And they're right. The solution, though, is not to wait for it or to go without it, but to create inspiration daily. From gardening to construction, even if you love your pursuit, inspire yourself first.

"This is the real secret of life – to be completely engaged with what you are doing in the here and now.
And instead of calling it work, realize it is play."
-Alan Watts

Seek inspiration before going to work. Even if it is a five-minute video of pretty birds, watch it before going to the shop to make birdhouses. Even if you are working for someone else, research ways to improve. Is there a glue or wood you shouldn't use? Are you making the holes too big— so big predators can get in? Is there a better type of nail? Do they need to be that deep? Which designs sell best on five of the most popular sites? What has the best reviews? After you find mentors and sources of inspiration, you will know how to become compelled to work out, write, or carve wooden statues. Pursue your goal, and flow from inspiration.

Often, we only seek inspiration in areas we are already skilled in. If you are strong in one area, it's partly because you've found inspiration and mentors there. But it's equally important to find these in areas you struggle with. If you're not a good lover to your wife, are snappy with your husband, or cannot seem to make or save money, look for those who can help you improve. Use inspiration from various sources to keep driving yourself toward your chosen goals. Finding a mentor to help you become more compassionate, healthy, and a better cook shouldn't only be on the list for those who already excel at these things. When you double what is working, and cut out what does not, don't neglect areas of your life that need attention or cut out something that has potential but requires effort to develop. Build on your strengths while also addressing your weaknesses.

You'll know you've truly applied this workbook when your life is so extraordinary that people you have never met often know who you are. It is huge to double what works and take out what does not until it becomes difficult to imagine how to do it again. When we know where we are and where we are going, we can get there. By refining our thinking and skills through writing, we surpass our current understanding of achievement.

We are creatures of habit; therefore, build the habits you want by applying everything herein over the coming days, months, and years. Habits—whether intentional or accidental—require no willpower to maintain. If you want to excel in training, business, relationships, and life, seek inspiration to create a workspace of flow and defeat doubts and difficult days before they even occur.

"The type of person you are is usually reflected in your business. To improve your business, first improve yourself."
-Idowu Koyenikan

Followers

Without loyal customers, you cannot create wealth. No matter how great your product is, it cannot sell itself. No matter how inviting a presentation, it won't matter if no one is there to see it and hear the story. From a shop to an online presence, prime locations are quite expensive since visibility equals visitors (not sales, but potential sales). Advertising effectively and in a pleasant manner for yourself and your customers, so long as it brings a return greater than the cost of marketing, is essential for success.

How many loyal customers do you need? Divide your desired yearly income (required for optimal happiness) by the average annual profit per loyal customer. Example: If your optimal yearly income is $240,000, and you make $50 profit per loyal customer per year, then you need 4,800 loyal customers. If you make $100 profit per loyal customer per month, then each one is worth $1,200 a year. Dividing $240,000 by $1,200 shows you need 200 loyal customers.

Number of loyal customers needed: _____

From a pool of online followers, around 1-5% of them will buy your products. Multiply the previous number by 100.

Number of followers needed: _____

> *"Action may not always bring happiness,*
> *but there is no happiness without action."*
> *-William James*

For each needed follower, you will need around 100 targeted <u>viewers</u> of your pitch. While this is a presumption, of course, you will need to research how many non-targeted viewers it takes to attract 100 targeted ones. Say you make and sell women's earrings. How many non-targeted viewers need to see your advertisement? Well, half of the population are women, sure, but, with research, you find that X% of them wear jewelry, but only X% prefer handmade jewelry, and X% of those have their ears pierced. This narrows the potential audience down to a fraction of those who might be interested. But I do not recommend this approach. Targeting your audience directly is far more effective than relying on randomness. If pursuing a non-targeted audience, do your own math, but if aiming for targeted customers, multiply the previous number by 50.

Number of online <u>viewers</u> who need to hear about my service to gain needed followers: _____

"If you trust in yourself, and believe in your dreams,
and follow your star, you'll still get beaten by
people who spent their time working hard
and learning things and weren't so lazy."
-Terry Pratchett

Next, we need to consider finding <u>replacements</u> for lost customers. People move or move on, after all. So say you need 100 students. How often does one quit? This tells you how often you need to replace one through repeated marketing efforts to maintain the number of students needed for optimal income.

Number of <u>replacements</u> of lost loyal customers needed per year? _____

In all of this, you need to have methods for people to find and then follow you!

Do you have an email list, a video channel, or a social media feed? Why not all three and more? This way, followers will be constantly reminded of your services. Someone who bought your first CD may never know about your second or third offering because they lack a way to keep up with you. This is their loss, as well as yours.

"I'm a greater believer in luck,
and I find the harder I work the more I have of it."
-Thomas Jefferson

While I dislike social media, it is still beneficial. From tried and true media sites to new platforms where you have a better chance of getting noticed, there are many avenues to take. In doing so, however, make sure you do not get lost. Use the media outlets. Do not let them use you by sucking away your time or causing you any stress. Find methods to make them enjoyable and easy to upkeep. And of all the platforms out there, which one caters most to your style of clientele?

Mimic what brought others success without blatant copying. For example, if a video titled, "12 steps for a huge tomato crop" has gotten a lot of views, can you use the skyscraper method to produce a better version? "23 steps for a huge tomato crop," or limit it and go into greater detail: "The only 6 steps you need for a huge tomato crop." Then make an even better cover image and clearer video that will direct traffic to your site, where you have even more information and offer tomato seeds and a starter mix.

"When bakers get together, they discuss art.
When artists get together, they discuss money."
-Oscar Wilde

How can you increase visibility among your target audience? Instead of generic radio ads, choose a program that aligns with your offerings. While you might not be able to get on a podcast that has millions of listeners, you can start with those that have a thousand subscribers and build your way up. This allows you to have, not just a 10-second ad, but an interview that could be listened to even decades later. From offering free classes to attending events where you will build grassroots connections in real-time, you must consider every opportunity to reach your audience. Whether it's interviewing for blogs, posting flyers, leaving business cards at businesses (with permission), or shooting the breeze with strangers, there are dozens of free or cheap ways to double your income by doubling regular customers, or even getting you your first customer. From sincere comments on social media platforms to visiting similar businesses so far away that they are not competitors (to see what works for them), start testing your list of methods to increase viewership.

Take an hour right now and write as many ways to increase visibility you can think of—no matter how obvious, vital, obscure, or silly. A quarterly email newsletter? A social media platform? Getting other newsletters to promote you? Whatever your ideas are, keep them brief. Write, "A brief easy-to-read sign" not, "Get a brand new, larger sign that is easier to read and maybe hire John to put it up."

Now, write beside each idea how you can use leverage it to achieve more in fewer hours. You can work 10 hours a day, but not 40, unless you hire employees. If your newsletter had a better sales pitch, could that turn 1% into 6% sales? Would it help to hire your feisty niece to ask customers at the farmer's market what their favorite desserts are to increase the value your bakery offers? From finding better leads to getting a large newsletter, podcast, or influencer to promote you, take your ideas and scale them from 10 to 100 to 1,000.

"The artist is nothing without the gift,
but the gift is nothing without work."
-Émile Zola

Some businesses don't have a sign, so locals don't know they exist. Others have advertising galore, but the ads might be silly or shady and you'll need to hire multiple consultants to give you better, or at least different, advice. Maybe you came up with more than 50 ideas, or, perhaps you only thought of five after an hour. If so, consider hiring someone to help develop your business strategy. Regardless, look at your ideas and circle your best five. Focus intensely on those for a full year. Watch videos, read blogs, buy books, attend seminars, and truly pour yourself into enhancing your ability to leverage these honest methods of letting others know there is an epic service or product. Yours! Next year, make another list, circle your top five, and continue reaching new followers.

"Be steady and well-ordered in your life so that you can be
fierce and original in your work."
-Gustave Flaubert

Spend this week, not learning why your five ideas won't work (because they can) or how to game the system, but research how to do these things professionally. Building a website may take the most time, and making videos may be the hardest and most nerve-racking, but put yourself out there anyway. While this may be difficult for those who are not hyper-social, doing them anyway will benefit your customers, yourself, and the charities a hero like you can help.

Note: Some want to do more, but limiting yourself to five ideas prevents spreading yourself too thin. It also allows you to become more proficient.

If there is a cost, find a way to minimize it. Test three ads that only air once to see if one outperforms the others. Rather than hiring a consultant for a year, hire one for an hour or a day and go from there. Do not pour everything into a single idea; instead, slowly increase your exposure while testing.

Some larger companies already have all the customers they will get from one avenue, so increasing the cost won't yield more. However, keeping it reminds people of their product. Everyone benefits by saying to their fans, "The nicest gift you could give us this holiday season is to let your friends know about our new music / menu / books. And we want to give this gift to you as well—go here for a free …"

It's never too early to start finding followers for your product or service. If you wait until your album's release to build a following, you may find a few, but if you start years beforehand, you could have tens of thousands of followers, which is the difference between selling a thousand copies and selling one—between a living wage and homelessness. While the saying goes, "Better late than never." the truth is, "Better early than on time."

Product Necessities

Some look at their great product and wonder why it isn't selling itself. No product sells itself! How many great products are out there that you do not know about but would buy if you did? It pays to improve your product, so long as you start and continue to find and keep loyal customers.

One of the best methods for turning **viewers** into **followers** into **loyal customers** is to have an outstanding product or service (again, provided they know about it) that is **ethical**, **legal**, **addictive**, and **fills a need** by addressing a lack your customer has.

"Don't judge each day by the harvest you reap
but by the seeds that you plant."
-Robert Louis Stevenson

Ethical? While taboo, it is fair to ask if your product is causing more harm than it needs to. Could you use repurposed wood instead of new, or adjust a recipe to incorporate greater kindness or sustainability? Genuinely evaluate what you are offering and see if you can make it more ethical than you feel is necessary.

Legal? Are you charging the right tax? Or should that be "taxes"? If you are shipping products, can this item be shipped in the mail? (Or for less?) What insurance do you need? Are you sure that is it? Have you spoken to a professional accountant and lawyer? Both are not just advisable but essential.

Addictive? I'm not talking about putting drugs in the tea you sell, but do you regularly offer new blends, new releases in a series, or something people want to buy again and again? The difference between a customer buying an item once versus monthly is extraordinary. Instead of one profit of $10, you have 12 profits of $10 each, or $120. May not sound like much until you calculate the cost of finding one customer. Consider the results of 1,000 customers buying once that year, providing $10,000 yearly, compared to 1,000 customers buying 12 times a year, yielding $120,000 yearly.

Fills a need? To be fair, if you don't have this, then you don't have anything. Why does your viewer want to become a follower? What value do they gain? Is there a free download, or is it because your service helps them stay healthy, happy, or even popular? Remember, no one sells products. They sell **stories** and **results**. The cliché here is that no one is in the market for a drill bit. What they really want is a hole in a piece of wood (result) so they can complete a project for their loved one (story). This is why when groups of college students come to the wineries to learn from me, I repeatedly say, "We do not sell wine. We sell ambiance." People come here to share a meal with family and friends, to walk through the gardens, and because the staff are nice. If the winery was a dump, no food was allowed, and the servers were rude—it wouldn't matter if our wine was the best in the world, we would be out of business in less than a year. We do not sell wine, but ambiance and stories. Now, for your business, write out, not the item, but the result and stories you provide:

Knowing this, write one sentence as your 10-second sales pitch for short conversations. To do this, draft 10 different ones on a separate paper and take the best aspects from each to craft a final version:

Can you easily speak for hours about what you provide? If not, my advice is to start acting a little crazy and talk aloud to yourself until you can. Afterward, find people who will listen and test your hour-long presentation about, not your product, but their results and story. Once you feel confident, find podcasts or record videos to reach tens of thousands of people who will be interested in your offerings.

> *"Hide not your talents, they for use were made,*
> *What's a sundial in the shade?"*
> *-Benjamin Franklin*

Of course, you must also explain why anyone would listen to you in the first place. Are you an expert because you have, well, have what? Did you write a book? Have you been a chef for 12 years? Do you have a degree? Are your works in 10 different locations? Even if small, be honest about your credentials, and find more and more ways (always) to let others know about your awesome goods or services. Otherwise, how will anyone hear the horn calling them to what could enrich their lives? If you are doing good business, then tooting your own horn is more of a service to others than to yourself.

From offering coupons and rewards for customers after X number of meals to a discount on their third painting, or free installation with the purchase of a warranty, find more and more ways to attract and keep loyal customers.

Whether it's hiring someone to make a logo or acquiring the rights to play better music at your venue, improve in ways that allow more people to fall in love with what you offer. Keeping customers is more effective than looking for new ones. And getting new ones? The best resource is the loyalty of your current audience. Encouraging your fans to tell others, with offers such as "bring a friend for free," or asking them to share this post or video. This tactic, if done tactfully, could double your followers and income.

"Work without love is slavery."
-Mother Teresa

Once more, let's say you have a new [insert whatever here] but zero people to contact, then what does it matter if you have something? Compare that to a list of 1,000 real people—I say "real" because there are a lot of dead or fake accounts out there, so do not get scammed. Now compare that to a list of 200,000 followers. Zero followers: zero sales. One thousand followers: tens of sales. Hundreds of thousands of followers: tens of thousands of sales. And with an impressive income, you can buy the wealth of continuing to pursue your impressive passions further than you have dreamed!

"We often miss opportunity
because it's dressed in overalls and looks like work."
-Thomas A. Edison

Will 4% of your fans know you have a new recording out, or a new dish on the menu? Will your friends know you have a new painting for sale, or are they in the dark, too? From friends at the gym to people you dance with, all the way to the Elder you met while hiking a mountain, gently let people know about the quality you offer. This isn't just self-promotion, it is a kindness to self and others.

"Without ambition one starts nothing.
Without work one finishes nothing.
The prize will not be sent to you.
You have to win it."
-Ralph Waldo Emerson

Success Can Lead To Failure

You might not think saving 10 minutes in your daily routine and an hour on a task once a week is significant, but that totals over 100 hours a year—time you could use for something productive. Pulling weeds with one hand? Double it and use two hands. Pulling weeds with two hands? Could you use a tool and go 27 times as fast? Using a tool? What if you use a mulch that blocks the weeds, saves water, makes plants grow bigger, and causes the garden to look even nicer?

Incorporate into your life the lessons in Removing Wasted Motion, Doubling Down, and Experimentation and Examination. Learn from all and become Inspired—sure, motivation doesn't last, but neither do baths. Pursue these with vigor to find all the Followers needed, offering a product that meets all Necessities.

Without emotional management, however, doing these things will only harm you! Do not neglect the other *Hero* volumes. Yes, even for a family you do not yet have, a community that does not yet value you, and a charity you do not yet know exists. To see all the workbooks, go to www.emotionalmanagement.org. Extra money for someone who is out of control can actually harm them. A drunkard or meth addict is still alive because they are broke. To no longer be broke, you must first no longer be broken.

"Money is only a tool.
It will take you wherever you wish,
but it will not replace you as the driver."
-Ayn Rand

*Damocles wished to have the opulence of King Dionysius.
The king asked, "Want a trial of my good fortune?" Damocles
agreed and was seated on a golden couch. Servants waited
upon him with food, wines, and perfumed ointments. But as
Damocles was about to enjoy the life of a king, he noticed
Dionysius had hung a sword above him, suspended by a
single horsehair. Now unable to savor affluence, he excused
himself, saying, "I no longer wish to be so fortunate."*

"Every man, woman, and child lives under a nuclear sword of Damocles, hanging by the slenderest of threads, capable of being cut at any moment by accident, or miscalculation ... or by madness."
-John F. Kennedy

What Is Money?

We often allow money, or the lack thereof, to cause our emotions to fluctuate from stress to greed. But let's look deeper at what we are seeking by asking: "What is money?" However, to answer any question anew, we must first get rid of old answers.

A gentleman once asked me to answer each question he asked as soon as I heard it. He asked, "What is money?"

I answered aloud, "The root of all evil." (It was a saying I had heard, and the first thing that came to my mind).

Then he asked the next question, which was the same! "What is money?"

I answered, "Hard to come by."

He asked it again, and again, and even though I did not know it would be the last time he would ask, "What is money?" I answered, quite honestly, with this:

"Happiness."

"Pleasure in the job puts perfection in the work."
-Aristotle

Money is not the root of all evil. That idea comes from misquoting the Bible. The Bible actually says, "greed of money is the root of all evil," and we would be hard-pressed to present a compelling argument against this. Money is simply an article of power, be it managed well or not.

I had to change my mental relationship with money. Money can pay for surgery, enable travel to see loved ones, and allow us to feed and be fed. This is not evil. But is it hard to come by? If not, then how do we acquire wealth?

In the temple, money-changers were selling doves to sacrifice,
forgoing the Scripture that states,
"I desire mercy, not sacrifice."

What were they really doing?
Doves represent peace.
Those in the temple were selling peace.

The Messiah drove them out with a whip, overturning tables,
shouting, "My house shall be called a house of prayer,
but you have made it a den of robbers!"

It is up to you, hero, to drive money-changers and sellers of
peace out of your heart. Peace, Love, and Hope, properly
capitalized, are free. Wealth is free, but only to those
who give value from an honorable heart.

Money's purpose is to function as a tool. Cash is merely a note that indicates value was given and appreciation was reciprocated. It is now an exchangeable note for other values. Hence, to make money so we can buy value, we must first provide a value. To do this, ask: "How can I provide value, be it a good or service, in a sustainable and recurring way? While enjoying the majority of what I do, how can I provide so customers feel they're getting more than they paid for?"

Ponder value (created from your effort) that results in a greater reward for your buyer. If you are painting, writing, gardening, or any of the like, it may be fun to dabble, and at times it will provide further education, but if you focus on one skill (only painting barns, for example), it will increase in value year after year. If you are even more specific (such as painting barns on old saws), you can develop unique expertise and therefore be in higher demand.

"It is a kind of spiritual snobbery that makes people think they can be happy without money."
-Albert Camus

While I will not share private details, I've received many messages. One spoke of how what I had shared about the harmful effects of pornography saved a couple's marriage. They were literally planning when to file for divorce. Now? Their marriage is wonderful, their children are happier, and their friends and family will not suffer from a separation. So when I make a few dollars working on these workbooks, I do not feel like a sellout. Your gain is higher than mine.

When someone builds confidence or is able to protect themselves through my self-defense classes, when a bird can fly once more due to my work with wildlife rehabbers, or even when I hear laughter at the vineyard while I work on the gardens and vines, I know I am providing value. You, likely, are also providing value—and when you can see that value, then, and only then, can you enhance your worth, thereby enhancing your wealth. And that isn't always money, sometimes wealth is a couple telling you they are more in love than ever before.

Now that you know where you are and where you want to go financially and are pursuing a path (passion) that brings you joy, set yourself a goal to double your current income.

If you are making, say, $33,000 a year, then the idea of making $12,000,000 next year is just so huge that your mind rejects it—you do not believe in that dream, so it stays a dream. If you are making $33,000, then the idea of making $33,001 is so easy you would not try, and there is no richness inviting you. But $66,000? That is possible, and you know it. You also know it will be a tough challenge, requiring effort, not once, but all year. There is no way you can achieve this by accident or by dreaming big. You need a plan you can follow and (the biggest takeaway of the whole workbook) act on. These sections will help you achieve this. So look back at Where You Are, write what you make per year, and double it. Know your goal!

Present yearly income: $_____

Goal for the next 365 days: $_____ (double the number above)

Value begets value. Remember this one phrase in all your dealings, and, if applied, you will always grow—financially, personally, and even spiritually.

Control Of Your Money

Money? Many say not to talk about religion or politics, but money is so taboo we don't even say not to talk about it—we just don't! You are not supposed to ask people how much they make, what they paid for something, and the like. If we discuss our wages, and you make more or less than I do, it often triggers nameless concoctions of emotions that are anything but pleasant.

So, how do we control money when we never speak about how to enjoy saving, how to avoid purchasing things in an attempt to fill a void, or how to make more money for the right reasons? As for control, though, perhaps the one person we need to talk about money with the most is ourselves.

> *"We may encounter many defeats*
> *but we must not be defeated."*
> *-Maya Angelou*

In losing control of our emotional grip on money, some challenges seem universal, while others may be more specific to you. When you shop for clothes, are you in control of your money, or do your emotions get the best of you? Are you buying that dress to feel loved or to instill jealousy in others, or is it about the S word: *Sale*? Many who struggle with this spend more than a gambler. When walking by charities, are you in control of your money—or is their ability to control your emotions a skill they have, but you lack? I've known people who donated so much that they had difficulty feeding their family, and others who refused to give to such a degree that there was a different kind of hunger in their household.

Write the last five things you bought that cost one to two days' wages:

1.

2.

3.

4.

5.

Now write beside each of those a few reasons why you bought these items. Do they still hold equal or greater value to their cost?

Below, write out five things, totaling near the same price as the above items, that would enhance your wealth by investing in yourself. Could it be video courses, therapy, a few kettlebells to get stronger, an old book on painting, or even something like a better cushion? Ponder this. What are the best investments you could make in yourself?

1.

2.

3.

4.

5.

We have emotional fear of money, and are easily manipulated by it! Control of money means seeing it and using it as a tool. To be in control of money, start by talking about it with yourself:

"Where do I lose control of money?"

"How can I regain control?"

For example, your struggle with gluttony may be easier if you make a list and battle temptation for the thirty minutes you are shopping rather than trying to have control all week with a pantry filled with goodies that aren't good for you.

"Every day is a bank account, and time is our currency.
No one is rich, no one is poor, we've got 24 hours each."
-Christopher Rice

I once had a rather odd but insightful conversation with myself. I know it is strange, but try this: Go to your closet and find your best and favorite article of clothing, as well as your most uncomfortable or worn-out garment. Lay them both on your bed. Go ahead.

Now, look at your entertainment—books, music, movies, you name it. Grab the least wholesome and the greatest work you have. Lay the worst next to the worst, and the best next to the best, on your bed and come back.

Reading and doing are two entirely different things. Go ahead—do these tasks. Often, we skip taking action, but, without action, no book will ever improve your life.

Ask yourself, "What makes me feel the worst after I have eaten / drank it?" Lay that by the other worst items. Then ponder what makes you feel the best—not for the moment, like a beer—but even the next day. Lay that on the bed, too.

Now, meditate for a few minutes while looking at these two collections.

See yourself.

Really see yourself.

In one pile, you're wearing unwanted clothing, engaging with things that weaken you, and consuming things that harm your health.

In the other, you're enjoying a great meal, seeing something that inspires you, and wearing clothes that make you feel confident and strong.

Now, take your time, and answer: Which version of yourself is richer? Which version should you invest in? The hero or the villain?

Control of money is control of self. This is about intentionally creating the person you want to be, rather than passively becoming someone you no longer wish to be.

"Out of clutter, find simplicity."
-Albert Einstein

Family & Friends

Being lonely is true poverty, but merely having people in your life is not the answer. When we lack friends, we often accept whoever comes along, but this can lead to poor relationships and a poorer us. The people who drink—they are fine folks, but if you want to grow then you need to find friends who don't. Find people who train body, mind, and soul—who have a physical passion, a love for learning, and a spirit of gratitude.

Possibly the quickest way to lose wealth is through poor choices in friends and partners. This has nothing to do with their income, and everything to do with their character.

My biggest hurdle in friendships and family relationships is that I am a giving person, making it easy for certain patterns to emerge:

Givers can be taken advantage of for their generosity. They may unknowingly use giving as a way to "buy" friendships, and are often deeply hurt when others don't give in return. This hurt can lead to bitterness and unintended consequences. We may become passive-aggressive, anti-social, or even resentful. We risk trading our genuine spirit of giving for a transactional mindset, expecting something in return from people who never agreed to that exchange. What we thought were gifts become, in our minds, down payments—ones others never wanted to honor.

That sounds dark and sinister because it is. Finding the best friends and partners, and spending time with the best family members doesn't just happen by chance. You have to aim for a known target, or you will never hit the mark.

To cultivate the wealth of meaningful relationships, define what that means by asking yourself:

What qualities must new friendships have?

What traits do I need to attract those people?

And what do I need to avoid so I don't repel them?

Tell that story here, but do so without trade or bitterness.

"Sorrow prepares you for joy. It violently sweeps everything out of your house, so that new joy can find space to enter. It shakes the yellow leaves from the bough of your heart, so that fresh, green leaves can grow in their place. It pulls up the rotten roots, so that new roots hidden beneath have room to grow. Whatever sorrow shakes from your heart, far better things will take their place."

-Rumi

Preparation For Peril

There is an idea that it takes 10,000 hours to become professional at a pursuit. While this is a decent guess, there are ways to hasten this approach, like a brisk walk instead of a slow pace. Learning from the best and working with a genuine desire to improve will, of course, help. But one thing helps most of all: the welcoming of pain.

Hardships will occur. That is all there is to it. One out of one of us will die. Everyone will become ill at many points. Cars and machines will break down, as will relationships and income. Sometimes, instead of one hardship, it is ten. And I know from experience that for some it isn't ten but an actual hundred hardships occurring within days. How well you handle this will determine how quickly you come back to the zeal you once had.

"You never know what worse luck
your bad luck has saved you from."
-Cormac McCarthy

Some start by dedicating an hour a day to their goals. When hardship strikes, they drop to zero hours. Meanwhile, someone putting in eight hours may drop to four hours. But the person who understands that pain is inevitable—who makes a pact with themselves to keep moving forward, even if their dream seems shattered—these are the people who come into wealth. Soon, the person who began with just an hour a day may bounce back and push themselves to two hours. While the one who did eight, now does twelve, using the hardship to become stronger in the long run.

Consider this: Do you tune instruments for bands? Will you stop if your girlfriend leaves you? Do you write poetry? Will your craft die if your husband dies? Grieve! Yes. But not forever, and not at the cost of what you love and what they once loved about you. Are you building your dream pizza parlor? What happens when your business partner, your only brother, cheats you, robs it out from under you, and leaves you homeless and sitting on the edge of a cot at a shelter? What then? Will you drop to zero hours? Will you give up? Or will you work hard at a job and even harder at making better recipes, and transforming your dream from a brick-and-mortar into a traveling pizzeria? Will you give up when the hardships come? Or will you tell a heroic tale?

Without preparation, hard times become disastrous, whereas, with absolute preparation, hard times can become a vacation. The first job I lost propelled me into my passions and self-improvement. I've seen the same situation destroy others, robbing them of self-respect and the will to look for new opportunities outside and within.

Times of peril are coming! You *will* get sick. You *will* lose your job. Your partner, statistically, has likely already cheated on you and is planning a separation—you *will* lose your loved ones, whether through betrayal or death. From fires to the common cold, from socialism to being wrongfully accused of a crime, we must prepare, but without it costing us joy in life.

"When defeat comes, accept it as a signal that your plans are not sound, rebuild those plans, and set sail once more toward your coveted goal."
-Napoleon Hill

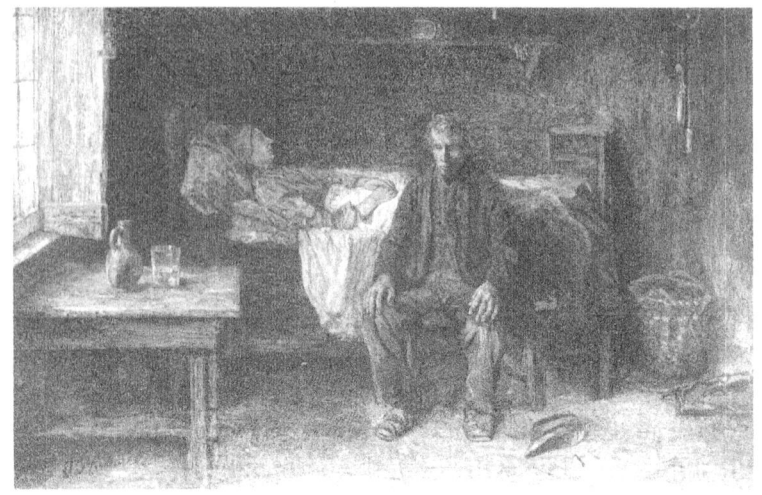

Alone.

Of all hardships, this is the most painful.

Losing a loved one, or never finding one.

Tribulation cannot fully be forgone.

But what of this painting? What if there, seated on the floor, the bed, and even leaning in the window, were the wealth of children and beloved friends and neighbors who mourn with you, and likewise celebrate the life of the one you loved most?

How differently can we paint life?

Or even death?

Buying a few top-end fire extinguishers may not prevent a fire—it may not even be able to save your house, but they have saved countless lives. Having a generator in certain areas has saved people from freezing to death or, at the very least, kept months' worth of food from spoiling. And what about insurance for health, life, and your dwelling? There are many avenues to consider when it comes to guarding against the upcoming storms of life.

In the 1980s, a well-known minister named Billy Graham was interviewed, and he stated that he never allowed himself to be alone in a room with a woman other than his wife. I, as well as the interviewer, thought that was too much. So Billy Graham continued to explain, saying (paraphrasing), "Even if one person said we were alone together and that I had acted inappropriately—this would tarnish my message of the Lord, and it is not worth the risk. Every person I meet with, I have deacons of the church and my wife with me." He then picked up a huge ledger and said, "I also record every meeting—their names, who was with me, the date, time, place, and what was discussed. Even if someone tries to accuse me, I have records and witnesses of my actions." That was decades ago, and the world is more dangerous in this way now. What can you do to enhance your safety?

"Shallow men believe in luck or in circumstance.
Strong men believe in cause and effect."
-Ralph Waldo Emerson

Sadly, I know a family who had their children taken away due to the kids playing rambunctiously, resulting in a bruise. Even though the children explained and the parents pleaded, social services took them away. The children were then molested by the step-parents before this family could get their children back. Some friends of these dear people now have video cameras in their own houses to protect themselves against the protectors.

Loss of a job is often another peril that cripples people. The majority live paycheck to paycheck. They do not have enough money to last a full month, let alone two. Missing one paycheck may mean they have to eat food they don't like, skip a drink, or walk to work. But two missed paychecks? They cannot pay for electricity, let alone their house.

Before you invest in stocks or real estate, your first financial goal should be to have a year's worth of income saved for hard times. Anyone who does not have at least three months' worth of savings should acquire another job, cut all non-essential expenses, and plunge themselves into saving as if peril were right around the corner.

It often is.

"If you had to identify, in one word, the reason why the human race has not achieved, and never will achieve, its full potential, that word would be 'meetings.'"
-Dave Barry

No one thinks their wife will cheat on them. Nobody thinks their husband will run off with the young babysitter. If they thought this, they would not have been with this person in the first place. And while it is best to guard yourself from becoming so reprehensible, and to actively communicate about and nurture your relationship, it is also wise to prepare for the unexpected.

Prenuptial agreements are not unromantic, but a sign of intelligence—you decide what to do at the height of love rather than the depth of loathing. Having a small safe at a trusted family member's home, bolted to the floor, fire, water, and theft-proof—with important documents, information, and enough cash to survive—is especially prudent for men, but is also wise for women. People acting loving still often cheat and leave—their actions can be crueler and more wicked than you would have ever imagined.

Recently, when selling a vehicle, I had a lot of people come to look at it. Every one of them were men who, one after the other, told me how they were trying to pick themselves back up after a bitter divorce—and how they so hoped that one year they would get to see their beautiful children again.

What about when someone dies? What about when *you* die? Worst case? You're dead. Are your children taken care of? Will some things remain private? What about that charity you love so much and that relies on your support? You left them, too.

Worst case? You start doing drugs. Your spouse becomes abusive. Your son commits suicide. Some things cannot be prepared for in full, but you need to think about these things and have discussions that could ultimately prevent some of them from happening. How many lovey-dovey, kissy-wissy couples talk about what they would do if one of them starts drinking too much, or if abuse comes into the relationship? "That would never happen to us!" is said by *everyone* it happens to.

The Ant And The Grasshopper, like Little Red Hen and
other similar stories, causes great discord and debate.
You would not think a children's tale about work
ethic could be so reviled, but here it is.

The ant works all summer, and the grasshopper mocks the
ant, for there is plenty, and so goes about playing polka.
When winter strikes and the grasshopper has nothing,
he then begs for food from the ant who worked. In some
renditions, the ant tells the grasshopper to eat polka or
to fill his belly with dance. The grasshopper dies,
not from starvation, but from laziness.

Some argue against the ant, calling instead for charity.
But not all charity is kind to the giver or even the receiver.
In reality, the grasshoppers would eat the ant's stores,
leading to famine for all, and would do nothing but
teach the grasshopper to come back again next year to beg,
or, if not that, to steal — at any cost but his own.

The other side of this? My family, harder working than any I know, through hail and drought, has gone without food. So hungry, they threw rocks at birds in desperation to eat. Grandfather was proud and refused help, but Christians came anyway and insisted – demanded – to give them food and clothing. Each of us has ancestors who lived from charity. It is right to give, but it is never right to harm in the process.

You need to be ready for a lot of strange things.

How prepared are you if all the stores close for three months? What about when they start denying you the ability to buy food unless you comply with new government regulations you cannot accept? Or will you just do as you're told until they march you off, too? The worst-case scenario can be much darker and stranger than you assume. "Never again?" Think again! History repeats itself. To deny this truth is to welcome war—a lamb's covenant with slaughter.

Only conduct business with friends and family if it is brief and low-risk. Sell them a book or car labeled "as is" for the full amount. Taking payments or selling an ongoing service will change the dynamic of your relationship—or ruin it should there be troubles. Often, people do not pay family or friends with urgency, and this, at the very least, creates stress. I would love to conduct business with people I love, but, since I love them, it is seldom worth the risk.

For some things, even the best preparation can't prevent them from becoming nightmares, thus we must also have prevention. Has a fire inspector checked your home? What causes most fires? How do most burglars get in? If you are married but not attending classes and workshops to improve your relationship, then you may first need to check with a doctor to make sure you are not clinically insane. If you understand how much you can lose or gain, then preparation for and prevention against all manner of peril becomes clear: Some buy money with wealth; others buy wealth with money. To be truly prepared, you must do the latter.

While renting may be better in some markets, there is a lot to be said about owning your home, having solar power, storing enough food, and cultivating the ability to grow your own food so you can survive any depression of the economy.

If, or rather when, paper money becomes useless, how wealthy are you? Do you have enough food for you and your pets? Enough toiletries to last a year, or maybe five? Do you have strong relationships with your community, friends, and family? Too often, we sacrifice time with loved ones in favor of entertaining ourselves, and, in doing so, we become poor.

> *"Ever tried.*
> *Ever failed.*
> *No matter.*
> *Try Again.*
> *Fail again.*
> *Fail better."*
> *-Samuel Beckett*

Do you have $5,000 saved but no longer have a connection with your uncle? Is, not your bank, but your garden account closed? What about your account of artwork, be that paintings or well-made clothes? And community is important! What value do you bring to your groups and town? Are you known for always bringing a goodie for a potluck at church? Do you bring a poem and flute to share at dance? Do neighbors know you as the person who pets cats and dogs, cleans up parks, and volunteers? A well-loved member of the community is often protected, valued, and rewarded by that community—even if in nothing more than the greatest wealth there is: love.

If you do not set a target, you miss your target. If you don't pick up your bow, you miss your target. If you don't draw back the arrow, aim, and loose, you miss the target. And if you do not find delight in progress—which many call failure after failure, day after day—you miss the target. All this requires an investment in failure. There is no other way! But what is the target? It is not an arbitrary number or set number you have discovered. It's life. It's the freedom to increase joy and decrease misery.

Something my Tai Chi Chuan instructor said often to the middle students was, "Invest in loss." Rather than mopping the floor with beginner students or fighting hard to win against advanced students, we were told to relax and allow both beginners and advanced to teach us—to see how they moved and how they would win.

Another truth he often shared came in the form of a question. "What is the first of the 8-Rules of Tai Chi Chuan?" And we would answer, "Relax." Then he would ask, "What is the second rule?" And we would answer, "Relax." You can probably guess what the other rules are.

Once relaxed and investing in loss, learn to see failure for what it truly is: an indicator of deviation showing exactly what you need to know. If the arrow hits too low, aim higher, or pull the bow back harder, or adjust your position. You are not sure yet, so you test and test.

> *"The strength of the team is each individual member.*
> *The strength of each member is the team."*
> *-Phil Jackson*

Success—what does that mean? When you hit the mark, or even close to it, do you feel joy? Whether it is playing cards or building a business, if there isn't a smile on your face, you are playing the wrong game. Silly, perhaps, but I don't smile when I win at certain board games. Yet, even when I lose liar's dice or the many types of poker I play with friends and family, I am smiling. Those are my games. When writing, even if I work all day and don't finish a page, I count my day as successful. Did I earn a dime? Ha! No. Do I rewrite it the next day? Yes. Do I get so lost in the process that sometimes I forget to eat, which I also enjoy doing? Yes. That is what the game should make you feel like. You could play this game of life all day every day and, in the end, lose by the world's standards, yet, on your deathbed, you'd know you spent your time doing what you loved. And if this is true, then we all want to share in your joy. You are not a sell-out. I do not consider a single artist in my library a sell-out. Instead of worrying about this, I urge you to:

Invest in quality tools before you dabble in bonds.
Invest in artwork before you trade stocks.
Secure provisions before acquiring properties.
Share smiles and connections, and you will find true wealth in your community of friends.

And when pain and loss come? Let it teach you and grow from it. The founder of Tae Kwon Do once said, "Pain is the best instructor, but no one wants to be his student." Learn from pain, but also prevent it—not by investing in comfort, but by investing in self-discovery and improvement.

"Try not to become a person of success,
but rather try to become a person of value."
-Albert Einstein

One of the greatest pains is unmet needs, which cause the biggest fights in relationships (from time together or apart, to money or trust). The solution? Mutually acted upon honest communication. One such conversation is something I once considered to be unromantic or even downright rotten. Now, though, it is painfully obvious that couples should have separate bank accounts for romantic and upright reasons. By doing so, a husband can actually take his partner out on dates and pay for the experience rather than it being a mutual bill. You can only buy your partner a gift with *your* money, not his or hers. If you want to buy X, it is up to you to earn it. If you go into debt, that is also your fault and problem—you are not a burden on others. It teaches us adults responsibility, which often diminishes after marriage.

Regarding children, it is equally important to teach them early on. If they work, they earn a little money, but they must learn how to spend it wisely. However, as simple as it is, if we want to teach our children how to live better lives, we have to first teach ourselves.

"The secret of change is to focus all of your energy,
not on fighting the old, but on building the new."
-Socrates

While so few relationships need to, most fail—but none of those men and women thought theirs would. And even those that last a lifetime, still end with loss. Whether through separation or the passing of a loved one, having separate accounts can provide simplicity during an already trying time. From prenuptial agreements, which should be mandatory, to writing down who owns what in wills, it is important to have all your affairs in order—and to have no affairs.

Just saying.

Having separate accounts is not only safer and more romantic; it also reinforces individual responsibility. Of course, everyone and every household is different. Some may ask, "What if the mother stays home to raise good children, tend the garden, and provide meals and hospitality? What about her income?" In this case, the husband should provide—not as a payment, but as a provision—by putting a set percentage of his income into her account. It should be half or more of his earnings—but that is just my opinion!

For this to work, couples must have these discussions when *very* calm. Take breaks at the first hint of frustration (as a mark of intelligence and honor), and decide what you both will do regarding everything, including money. If one partner falls prey to overspending, be it through gambling or donating, the household is not ruined if your house is in order. These situations happen too often to ignore prevention.

From using software to prevent identity theft to being careful in choosing a partner, take steps to enhance your safety without sacrificing your enjoyment of life.

Hero, Vol. 5 goes over finding a relationship, being in one, and navigating separation (death or non-mutual choice). This book, a trilogy of sorts, has been a long time in the making. While it will not have all the answers, I know it will have enough to propel you into a better life. Imagine living a life where your biggest heroes (your spouse and children) saw you as their biggest hero, too. Funny little thing, isn't it, that we can get what we dream of, so long as we dream clearly and aim with both heart and mind. Yet, what good is money without a kind heart? And what is a kind heart with nothing to offer loved ones? Keep improving, my dear friends.

"To get the full value of joy
you must have someone to divide it with."
-Mark Twain

A dishonest shortcut to the arch of fortune, be that of money or love, always comes back for you. Without the right path tread, we will not be the persons we need to be once we've arrived. When an honest wealthy man loses his wealth, within a few years, he has it again. When a poor man is given money, soon he is poorer than when he started! The path matters! A man who believes he can find a good wife will do the work to become a good man. A man who does not believe he can find one doesn't even bother to ask. All actions stem from belief. Believe in yourself and the value of honest work!

Windfalls

A lot of people receive one or more windfalls of money in their lifetime. These can range from the unlikely, such as winning the lottery or stumbling upon it, to the more common, such as inheriting it, receiving a large bonus, or selling a house. Windfalls, though, often do more harm than good. Family, friends, and charities will almost attack you while requesting money. And many who receive a large sum of money end up spending it all at once, leaving themselves poorer than before, or in debt due to unknown taxes.

To avoid these pitfalls, establish rules before a windfall ever happens. Also, identify what a windfall is for you. For me, it is anything over one month's wage. My rules are these:

Do not touch 90% of the windfall for one year, unless there is a life-or-death emergency, such as medical care that cannot be afforded otherwise. The remaining 10% of the windfall may be used within the year for bills and enjoyment. However, if there are outstanding debts then all the money goes toward paying them off. Afterward, if I don't yet have a year's worth of savings, I must be responsible and put that windfall aside to prepare for future hardships.

"Life is a shipwreck,
but we must not forget to sing in the lifeboats."
-Voltaire

I also check to see how much in taxes must be paid, and if there are ways to remove or reduce them, whether through legal deductions, loopholes, or charitable donations.

If the windfall is sufficient, I'll consult a financial adviser who can direct me to Roth IRAs, 401(k)s, or help set back a high-interest fund for future education or retirement.

When deciding what to spend the money on the following year, I prioritize needs, such as home repairs or tools to support my passions. But I also consider long-time wants, like trips or experiences that could bring joy to me and my loved ones. It is fair to enjoy life, after all.

Guard yourself against "get-rich-quick" and "invest right-now" schemes. There'll always be good investments—as well as poor ones—and we do not know which is which.

Do not give any to friends, families, or charities for the first year. Tell them the truth, "I am not touching that money this year. I want to use it intelligently and not be swept away. I will not give any of it to anyone. I know that sounds harsh, but I will be your friend—never a bank." This seldom causes a loss of friendship, whereas giving money often does unless you give the same amount to everyone, and even then!

Keep your job and continue to work. Even if the windfall is so huge that you could retire right now, don't. Work for at least another month, and if you part ways, make sure you do so with honor. And make sure, triply sure, that the windfall is 100% yours—not just on its way, held up in courts, or only half the amount after taxes. Keep your job and honor. You can't buy new honor.

Finally, look to the future. How long will this money last? Consider inflation, a long life, and unforeseen hardships. If you live 50 more years instead of 40, get burned in a divorce, sued by a driver, and have three surgeries, what then? Preparation for peril, as well as windfalls, is essential to basic money management.

"The most common way people give up their power is by thinking they don't have any."
-Alice Walker

In addition to these, what other methods might you utilize when receiving a windfall? If it is small, what will you do with it? Will it be a fund for a car replacement or a bunch of new video games that cost $2,000 in cash and $14,000 in time? This, like all matters in life, is up to you, but make the decision when calm and rational, not after a windfall has already swept you. Have an anchor for when your ship does come in. Write your plan here:

"Everything can be taken from a man but one thing:
the last of the human freedoms — to choose one's attitude in
any given set of circumstances, to choose one's own way."
-Viktor E. Frankl

Intermission

Some of the greatest gifts that I have received were compliments so intensely powerful that they went from ego-boosting to humbling. Others were handwritten cookbooks or collections of sayings. From a favorite bowl to a nearly worn-out tool, these gifts were life-changing for both the giver and the receiver.

This is why the Elders I know slowly give away their belongings to family and friends. My bookcase overflowed into another and another until I began giving books as gifts— even my favorite ones, some of which I have dozens of.

If this book helps you gain wealth, then it will not diminish your wealth—let alone your money—to buy a copy for a friend, or the series for your children. If this, or indeed any book, has helped turn you into a hero, then do the noble thing and share that book with as many people as you can!

"When I have a little money, I buy books;
and if I have any left, I buy food and clothes."
-Desiderius Erasmus Roterodamus

Investing & Reinvesting

Keep it simple by turning making money into a game, seeing how much you can save each week or month. But how do we invest and get a good ROI (return on investment)?

If you invest in stocks, follow these rules:

Be okay with losing all the money.

Do not invest in anything if you'll ever need that money.

Do not invest to make money—hope that it will, but focus on supporting something you truly care about. If you love the sea, invest in companies that aid the sea. If you are a fan of electric cars, invest in those.

And last: Play the long game. Do not invest in something and hope to sell it tomorrow, next month, or next year. I knew a fellow who invested in the railroad many decades ago because he loved trains. His small investments turned into hundreds of thousands. Yet, he was devastatingly poor. All he did was smoke and watch TV. No friends. No health. A hero to no one. He was one of the poorest people I've ever met.

It's better to start by investing in yourself—whether through books, hiring help, or purchasing high-quality tools.

Three better investments might look like:

1. You spend $20.00 on a book about your passion, such as how to tend flower bulbs.

2. Rather than buying a hedge trimmer and ladder, and fighting with it to try to level your unruly hedge, you spend $150.00 to hire a professional.

3. When shopping for a seat to roll around in a garden with, rather than getting the static one, you spend three times as much and get the adjustable one that has a nicer pad, and even spend an extra $10.00 to get it in the color you want.

Now, let's look at three wrong investments:

1. You don't know anything about the stock market but invest $100.00 into cheap stocks, or ones you just know (somehow) will be great.

2. You go to a bargain store and buy a dozen books for $30.00, but then never read them.

3. You get a stereo put in your car for $150.00 so you can listen to the radio on the way to work.

> *"The best investment*
> *is in the tools on one's own trade."*
> *-Benjamin Franklin*

Which of these two cases will give you the most enjoyment, and best ROI?

Who'd not rather own one great pan than a dozen cruddy ones? I'd rather enjoy my work and have a side job to make enough than work myself ragged just to buy stuff I don't need, to impress people I don't know, who are also doing the same thing and aren't paying attention anyway! I'd rather be paid in smiles and changed lives than stress and mere change. And I bet you would, too.

> *"Faith and fear both demand you believe in*
> *something you cannot see."*
> *-Bob Proctor*

How many of us never see results because we fail to invest in our craft, marketing, or personal growth? What else could bring in more money? What about investing in ways (not singular) to attract new customers, retain loyal ones, enhance your sales staff, and make your business shine so people can find it and enjoy your service?

Reinvesting into your business or passions should follow a clear plan with either a set amount or percentage of income. If you are not yet making a living from it, start by setting aside one to three day's wages per month. If you are making half a living or more, switch to 20% of the income it brings in, then increase it by 10% every quarter until you're redirecting 50% of your profits back into the pursuit. Even in a restaurant, keeping your regulars happy is priority number one—they keep you in business! But doubling their number should be a close second.

But what about investing in digital money, gold, or other hard assets? Soft currency, like cash, can be produced at will, which reduces its value (your buying power) every time more of it is printed. Gold, alternatively, cannot be manufactured. There is a limited amount found per year (roughly 1% of the total amount) and has always had a purpose that outweighs supply. (Silver, copper, and iron are easier to find and replace). Rare [insert anything here] always has value. Rare comics, stamps, or even seashells retain their value. Some digital companies, like Bitcoin, cap the number of digital coins produced, while other e-coins lack such limits, enabling insiders to make fortunes at the expense of others. But even these have all seen legal issues. As with any investment, you must be willing and able to lose it all.

> *"Act according to your principles,*
> *not your mood."*
> *-Goethe*

So what investments have given you the biggest ROI? Was it your gym membership? A wedding ring? Did a book change your life? Reflecting on your best investments can help you identify other great opportunities to reinvest. For example, it may inspire you to buy gifts for your partner, explore other books written by that author, or the like. Take your time to ponder and discover at least 10 of the best investments you've ever made:

1.

2.

3.

4.

5.

6.

7.

8.

9.

10.

Again, do not invest just for money. I would never invest in pornography, oil, or perfume companies because I do not like them. I'd rather lose money and save my soul by investing in compassion.

When investing, though, understand the difference between assets and liabilities. One makes you money while the other one drains it. Yet, it is risky to bet in a card game you've never played and have no idea what the rules are. There are mild gambles, such as investing in tax liens, to large gambles, such as playing the lottery.

I bought tax liens once. I went in, thinking it was great. The weather was so bad that I thought no one would show up. It was down-pouring with winds so strong they would darn near knock you over. Turns out, everyone thought the same thing. The place was packed. The liens all went for much higher than everything I had read on it and expected. There were about forty liens for sale, and I only bought one because it was the cheapest one at double what I was advised to pay. In the end, I was one of two people who made any money on it. The taxes on the one I bought were not paid until the last moment. The other person, though, actually got the house he bought the taxes on. He then fixed it up and rented it out. He won that odd rainy day lottery, I made out okay, but everyone else lost money. It was a gamble I have not done since, but may again in the future.

It is said you should buy when others are afraid and sell when others are at peak greed. But this only works if you know what to buy and sell—and even professionals don't always get this right!

Stocks are great if you take the time to understand them. But if you already know or enjoy the violin more, learn how to invest in it instead. Two friends of mine know the brands, understand the sound, and buy, repair, and sell violins and cellos. They treat those items like stocks—buying 10 for a thousand and selling them for ten thousand! Listen to your friends tell you about how their shares went up 5%, be happy for them, and then continue doing what you love. That is real wealth. If you still want to invest in stocks, first play a game:

Most people play a fool's game and say, "If I had invested in these stocks, I'd have this much money now!" They do not look at the thousands of stocks that failed. Instead, play a smart game and practice investing on paper. For the next year, set aside the real money you would need to invest in these stocks (or items, metals, coins), leaving it all in a savings account. Pretend to invest each week or month and, at the end of the year, calculate your returns honestly. Did you gain 11% or lose 46.8%? You may choose to play this game for a couple of years before investing real money, ensuring you understand more and are okay with the possibility of losing it all.

Some wish they would have bought into Bitcoin early on—same with Apple, Microsoft, and Tesla. Of course! But I've invested in other companies and digital coins that were once on the up and up, only for their value to drop to pennies. So rather than kicking myself for this, I have decided to only dabble in that which I enjoy. And in that dabbling, I am 100% fine with losing each investment. Even the best investor faces losses. I know I'll lose many, if not most, of the investments I make. This means returns from great investments must be weighed against losses from those that weren't great. Hence, a 19% return, after factoring in losses, may only be a 1.9% return—if a return at all. In this, I find the next section to be a much more reliable way to earn money with your money.

Buying & Selling

When the internet was starting to become huge, I posted paper flyers in banks, gas stations, and various businesses within a two-hundred-mile radius, saying I was looking for a Bowflex. This exercise machine sold online for around $1,400, but people sold them offline for $600 to $800. During this time, I had a decent job, making $350 a week. By buying and selling two to three Bowflexs a month, I could make a living wage. Instead of making $1,400 in 20 days of work each month, I made roughly $2,000 in 3 days of work each month. This was 100% interest—per month!

Imagine if your bank gave you 100% interest on your money. Wouldn't you want to put in everything you could? I mean, 100% interest would make many people sell their cars to put the money into that epic account. But what if you bought your car for a deal, and then listed it and sold it down the road for double? Isn't that 100% interest?

"It's the start that stops most people."
-Don Shula

Buying items on sale or in bulk, and reselling them, is a core principle for most businesses. I once worked for a seed company where the owner bought 50-pound bags of garden seeds and used simple machines to pack the seeds into tiny sealed packets. We would then put forty of these different seed packs into a larger bag and sell them. Our customers got a great deal on that many seeds. But the company? The profit margin was too ridiculous to mention. Even then, when the owner found a deal on the packets we used, he bought a truckload, resulting in more than $100,000 in extra profit that year—more than all the employees made!

A friend of mine makes about $1,500 a month by refurbishing free furniture she finds on online marketplaces, garage sales, and sitting outside people's homes with a sign that reads, "Free". She brings the pieces to her garage, sands them, stains or paints them, and then sells them online. $1,500 is what some people make working a job they hate.

My friend who sells furniture has a different approach to the things she owns: all of it, and I mean all of it, is for sale— if the price is right, of course. Even her house was for sale, at a higher price than it was worth, and after two years, it sold. She lists everything, and if it sells, great, and if it doesn't, great. This approach reinforces that stuff is just stuff, and helps her see everything as an investment. For many, this is intense. Would you sell your [insert anything here]? If you bought it for $20, and someone offered you $40, why wouldn't you sell it? You could always buy another. The stuff you own more than likely owns you instead. Put a price on everything you have and see it for what it is: stuff.

Another friend of mine sells laptops and computer gear. Going to sales at brand name stores, he buys, for example, the $1,400 laptop that's on sale for $999. He stacks discounts by using coupons from the computer company, taking advantage of a percentage off for signing up for a store program, and earning 5% cash back by using the store's credit card. He also negotiates with the store for an additional discount if he buys them all, thus getting him an even better deal. The price would often drop to $900 or even less. He would travel all day, going from store to store, buying them all, and then listing them online for $1,350 since that is what they were selling for. The buyers were happy to save $50 or more, and my friend made around $400 to $500 profit from each sale. And he would sell around five laptops a day. He made more profit in one day than most people do in a month. Granted, he searched for tricks to reduce price, learned what sold and for how much, and understood the product.

From wineries buying grapes to make and sell wine, to soap makers turning ingredients into bars of soap, there are near-infinite possibilities of buying and selling.

"You are the only problem you will ever have and you are the only solution. Change is inevitable, personal growth is always a personal decision."
-Bob Proctor

Buying wealth with money means buying time—time to be with family and friends. From 100-year-long studies by Harvard to National Geographic's article on super-centenarians, we know longevity and joy do not come from numbers in a bank account, but from nurturing close relationships. Sell a kitchen tool or painting, but never sell family and friendships short by being too poor to visit or too busy trying to get rich. Family. Friends. Those are real riches.

Some things you can buy and sell are strange. I have seen decks of playing cards from a film sell for $5.00, but after they were discontinued, the same cards routinely sold for $100. Go ahead and try to get that level of return from a bank or a stock. From baseball cards to comics, from signed photos to beer steins, there's a vast range of collectibles and necessities that can double your income if you first learn the market and then start.

From buying paintbrushes at a going-out-of-business sale to buying books at library sales and then reselling them online, what are 20 things you could buy and sell for a profit?

1.
2.
3.
4.
5.
6.
7.
8.
9.
10.
11.
12.
13.
14.
15.
16.
17.
18.
19.
20.

"Get your ideas on paper and study them.
Do not let them go to waste!"
-Les Brown

Now, put a checkmark by the best three after considering these questions:

What percentage is the profit?
Is the hourly profit double the value of your current wage?
Will it be indefinitely repeatable?
Is it ethical to yourself and others?
Are the items small or easy to transport?

Now, try the best one by investing very little at first. See what you can do. Even if not wholly enjoyable, the profit could help you build your dreams of wealth.

The best things to sell, though, are your creations. Yet, how do we price those so we can keep customers, make a living, and not feel as if we are robbing people?

Pricing

Free, low-price, middle-price, and high-end items are the backbone of all businesses. From food to art, from counseling to piano lessons, it is best to offer items in each range to optimize monetization and the ability to share your work with others.

"I challenge you to make your life a masterpiece.
I challenge you to join the ranks of those people who
live what they teach — who walk their talk."
-Tony Robbins

Imagine a lawyer who gave free legal advice once a month, or made videos about how to avoid bankruptcy, divorce, or lawsuits. Do you think he would have more business for doing so? And, above that, the wealth of more respect from the community?

Or consider an artist. Her paintings are incredible! But a framed acrylic piece might cost thousands—well beyond what most people can afford. So, to make her work accessible to a wider audience, her pricing strategy might look like this:

Free: Epic-looking business cards, downloadable computer wallpapers, and videos where she talks about her inspiration, life, and the like.

Low-Price: For those who like her artwork and want to support her, but simply cannot afford much, she offers small, affordable items like decals featuring her artwork for car windows or lockers, postcards, small posters, or gift sets that allow people to choose three of any. It is fun, brings in fans who will remember her work, and makes a bit of money, too.

Middle-Price: Wall scrolls, framed prints, classes, advice on where and how to display art at home, and live paintings at events that could draw in more customers while showcasing her talent.

High-Price: Original artwork or custom commissions, such as a tarot deck or church mural. While these high-ticket items, may only sell a few times each year, they account for half of her living. But only half.

Restaurants follow a similar approach: Free chips and salsa, tea, or after-dinner mints. It should at least be better than tap water so cold you can't taste the impurities brought to you in a plastic cup. Then there are low-priced appetizers, middle-price meals, and high-end menus available upon request (so the price doesn't scare anyone off). They may also offer private dining, expensive drinks, or catering.

"Success is not the key to happiness.
Happiness is the key to success.
If you love what you are doing, you will be successful."
-Albert Schweitzer

If you sell 100,000 items at $10.00 each, that is one million. But raising the price to $11 adds an extra $100,000. Or would that increase cause sales to drop by 20%? Testing is imperative. Even those who only offer free stuff can list items for sale through affiliate marketing, selling high-ticket, mid-range, or low-priced items that can still help people while bringing in a few dollars. Even a page asking for donations could be worth testing.

Without income, you cannot dedicate much time to your pursuit, a pursuit others get to enjoy. Yet, there is no reason to not increase your wages at work, too.

Increasing Wages

They say you make 40% more if you work 10% more than needed. Is this true? For most people, no. You'll make much more than a mere 40%.

I once worked with a family who split rent and bills. All three of them were consistently late for work by at least 15 minutes, and would often leave early, sometimes even an hour early. Every week, they were waiting for their paychecks. They needed that money for food and bills. No one had any savings at all. On the low end, skipping 30 minutes of work daily adds up to an hour and a half of lost wages per day between them all, which is seven and half hours per week, and 30 hours per month. If they had worked those extra hours and put all that income aside, they'd have nine extra full paychecks each year to put toward savings, paying off old debts, and living a better life.

But let's take it further. The amount they spent on smoking and drinking, both alcohol and pricy sugary drinks, in and of itself would have been (and yes, I did the math) over 16 extra paychecks per year. And that is a low figure.

Now imagine how much more they could have earned in raises for being trustworthy employees. How much better could they have performed their jobs if they were healthy—or at least not digging their own graves? Another 10 paychecks a year? More? Regardless, that is 35 extra paychecks per year for that family. Even if it was just one person, that is still over 10 extra paychecks each year!

"The more your money works for you,
the less you have to work for money."
-Idowu Koyenikan

137

While it is said that you make 40% more by working 10% more than needed, for those who used to only save an hour's wage (if that), the difference is much greater. Consider someone who hardly saves anything while making $500 a week. By the end of the year, 10% more is an extra $5,000. Ten years is, of course, $50,000. And that is all from merely being a decent employee. Zero savings compared to thousands cannot be measured in percentage, but if it could, it wouldn't be a meager 40%.

I also think of this in regards to empty calories. A once-upon-a-time favorite beer of mine has 160 calories (no protein, vitamins, or anything of value). One six-pack a week equals 49,920 pointless calories a year—not to mention it costs a week's worth of work, countless hours of downtime, and passions not pursued.

"When you work on something that only has the capacity to make you 5 dollars, it does not matter how much harder you work — the most you will make is 5 dollars."
-Idowu Koyenikan

Becoming a better employee unlocks free time, vacations, and a better quality of life. Offering a variety of price tiers your followers would want, creates wealth, for both your audience and you. Yet, without action, you'll never succeed. This is where everyone goes wrong. It is the only way you will fail—not falter, but fail!

How much can you save each year by getting rid of harmful habits, ranging from empty calories to lost hours:

Year-end total $_____

If you put in an extra half hour at work a day, and, after learning how to do a better job, asked for and received a 50-cent raise for the last half of one year, how much extra would you make?

$_____

> *"Nothing is really work unless you would*
> *rather be doing something else."*
> *-J.M. Barrie*

Now, make a list of what you can offer for free, low, middle, and high prices. Then underline what you are already doing, and circle the things you are not:

Free:

Low Price:

Middle Price:

High Price:

Read over the above and place an asterisk by one item from each list that you are going to get up and work towards right now before continuing in this workbook.

I know this will sound harsh, but there is no point in reading if you don't apply what you learn. May as well not bother learning anything at all. If you are not willing to try, then you may need the other workbooks in this series more so than this one.

Regardless, if you cannot be of value to your employer, you may as well forget about being valuable to your followers, customers, or guests. You did nothing but waste your time reading this unless you apply it, so do it now.

You can succeed! Others have, so there is no reason why you cannot, unless you give up before you even try.

Remember, products, no matter how great, do not sell themselves. You must market them relentlessly. Complete this section before reading on.

"There's no shortage of remarkable ideas,
what's missing is the will to execute them."
-Seth Godin

When & What To Be Paid

An old religious text (Torah) states an employer cannot withhold an agreed-upon wage for even a day. This would teach us a lot about money. Paychecks usually consist of one to two weeks of pay all at once, making us used to windfalls of cash. Receiving a daily wage means we must save each day or we will not have anything (any windfall) for rent.

An agreed-upon wage?

Minimum wage is a touchy subject for people, and many erroneously think they want it to be increased. Let's say that minimum wage is $10, and it increases to $20. The shirt you buy for $10—will it stay $10? Of course not! It won't increase to $20 either. That shirt will now cost $21 to $23 because not everyone in the supply chain earns minimum wage. The company also has to do two things. First, it has to find a way to reduce labor costs, whether through replacing workers with machines or by sending the job to a cheaper factory overseas, both of which have significant initial costs. Second, consider this: If the company had $200,000 in savings, the spending power of that money is now less than half (since everything costs more, including the employees). To recover, not just the money but its spending power, the employer must increase the price of the product, and, in many cases, make the product with cheaper materials. These changes lead to job losses, declining product quality, and long-term harm to our country and the people who live here.

Wages should be negotiated between the employer and employee. There are infinite jobs out there! My neighbor could not afford to pay someone $20 an hour to help with yard work, but she could pay $5. And there have been many times in my life when I would have gladly accepted a $5-an-hour job—especially if it comes with a meal and homemade cookies! And now I could afford to buy cheap but healthy food for my household! … Or the government can print funny money, that we will, in taxes, have to pay back many-fold.

And worse?

Our Elders—the ones who built the homes and towns we live in, who made the recipes we enjoy, and played the songs our memories hold dear—their savings are halved, and their Social Security doesn't go up. Meanwhile, their cost of living more than doubles.

Our system is not properly structured. Therefore, you need to have safeguards in place. While saving money is wise, it's even wiser to cultivate wealth in the form of family, friends, community, food, and physical resources.

"Trust isn't just the greatest currency,
it's the only currency. Once trust is gone in
any form of currency, the value is gone."
-Richie Norton

Who To Hire?

I am amazed at how many people advertise that they will not hire someone unless they have experience. If they have experience, why are they not still at their old job? But more than this: People are hired because of their education, experience, or maybe they are a friend of a friend, but they are fired because of their personality or lack of tenacity. As a business owner, instead, hire people who love doing what you do. This makes me think of something my boss once told me: "You know what I like about you? You actually care! I don't have to tell you to do most things because you just see a need and do it. You pick up trash even if it is out of your way and do the dirty jobs without complaints. And most of all, you call customers our guests and treat them as such. If I had a big company, I would make you the manager and never worry." A great compliment. And that is something to consider if you're doing the hiring. Even if not a passion of theirs, can they at least bring passion to the project?

Interviews should be in three parts:

Paperwork.

Conversation.

One hour of volunteer work at your job.

If they show zeal, hire them, even if they're not yet good at the job.

"If you hire people just because they can do a job, they'll work for your money. But if you hire people who believe what you believe, they'll work for you with blood and sweat and tears."
-Simon Sinek

Same goes the other way, too. If you are looking for jobs, interview places without them knowing about your intention. Go to that restaurant and order a meal. Is the staff friendly? Ask them how they like working there. If it is just a job to them, enjoy your meal, leave a tip, and try somewhere else. Find a place where the employees give rave reviews about their boss and the environment. It is massively important to find great people to work alongside—while being the best person and worker you can be and understanding that dealing with unruly guests, coworkers, and even a grumpy boss from time to time is part of your pay.

"Somebody once said that in looking for people to hire, you look for three qualities: integrity, intelligence, and energy. And if you don't have the first, the other two will kill you. You think about it; it's true. If you hire somebody without [integrity], you really want them to be dumb and lazy."
-Warren Buffett

When working for someone, always provide more value than they've asked for. When hiring, keep only those who consistently provide more value than expected.

When working at a company (or even for yourself) ask these two questions:

"Would I pay someone double my wage for the work I just did this past hour?"

"Is anyone here outworking me?"

You are being paid to create a profit for the company. Many employees don't even earn their keep, meaning other workers are carrying their load. If you want to be wealthy—valued!—make sure you are a part of the team. The company you work for is your boss's dream. Be a part of that dream or find something else to do. Ask, even if self-employed, "Am I earning my wage? Could I outwork the me of yesterday?" Strange to ponder, but could you achieve double or triple what you achieved in that hour? Are you earning money or is this busy work? Find ways to outperform yourself and you'll never be caught by those who don't.

Ownership of emotions grows when taking responsibility for yourself by working a physically demanding job—even if you are wealthy. Pursue your art, yes, but you still need to work for the community in which you live. That simple act of building character and emotional strength is something we should never sacrifice for convenience or ease. In this, the employer should also be a good employee.

"Every person needs to take one day away. A day in which one consciously separates the past from the future. Jobs, family, employers, and friends can exist one day without any one of us, and if our egos permit us to confess, they could exist eternally in our absence. Each person deserves a day away in which no problems are confronted, no solutions searched for. Each of us needs to withdraw from the cares which will not withdraw from us."
-Maya Angelou

Free Money: Debts To Savings

Times and circumstances change. If your company matches what you put into a 401(k), then pouring money into that is wise. But you may be a farmer working for yourself. If so, visiting extension offices, connecting with other farmers, and searching online may help you find subsidies, programs, grants, or other measures to help your farm. One year, there was a program that paid people in a certain region a small amount of money for every tree they planted, so long as it survived at least five years. A few farmers took advantage of this and planted a few tree rows. One of them, however, planted 100 times more than any other farmer, and, by doing so, paid for his farmland and new house! For others, maxing out a Roth IRA can help defer taxes and increase wealth. All opportunities change regularly, so no single book can cover every possibility.

"If you want to stand out from the crowd,
give people a reason not to forget you."
-Richard Branson

Others need to find, not one way, but 10 ways to consolidate debts. These ways, too, will change.

A friend of mine had one failed business after another, had bought a house he couldn't afford, had things in storage he didn't need, and a large family he loved—life was chaos, and bills were all marked final notice. So he did something risky, but it worked! He got a bunch of credit cards that had high spending limits with 6 months of interest-free charging. He paid many of his debts using these cards. He also liquefied unwanted belongings to help pay other debts. Then, however, he had tens of thousands of debt on cards with horribly high interest. But during those six months, he was able to pay off debts he had at other locations. He then talked with the credit card companies, saying, "Look, I cannot afford to pay this all at once, and the interest is killing my family. If I write you 6 checks for the full amount, each dated a month down the road from the other, would you consider that payment in full and stop charging me interest? Otherwise, you can just keep sending me notices I can't—and won't—pay." Some agreed, and he paid them off that way. The others were moved to new credit cards.

Fortunately, with another six-month history of consistent payments, he was able to transfer his remaining credit card balances to a debt consolidation company at a much lower interest rate—dropping from 20% to 8%. Then, using new cards, he paid that company off. Six months later, he then switched to another debt consolidation service. Through hard work, buying and selling, and cutting unnecessary expenses, he gradually turned his financial situation around. It took him nearly six years of juggling, but he did it. Now, the money that once went mostly to interest and some to debt repayment is being poured into education for his children and travel with his wife.

In some places, you can't do that legally, though. And risky strategies can backfire.

"You see things; you say, 'Why?'
But I dream things that never were; and I say, 'Why not?'"
-George Bernard Shaw

If you are in debt, ask yourself this: What are the smallest expenses causing debt? And I mean the tiniest! Is it a subscription that costs only $4.50 a month? You might think that $54 a year isn't that big of a deal, but think how happy you have been when you find a $20 bill on the road, or even a $1 bill. There are a lot of places we can find free money. What if you found a way to reduce the interest on a loan by 1%? Maybe you can't today, but by improving your credit score by paying bills a few days before their due date, in time you may be able to ask for an interest reduction. For some families, this could translate into many thousands saved.

From carpooling and turning off lights to lowering the thermostat by 1 degree, there is free money everywhere. Write out 12 expenses, from tiny to large, that may offer ways to save or find free money. Do you really need that streaming service all summer, or is that more of a winter thing? What if you could save a few hundred on vehicle expenses by getting better gas mileage, insurance, or the like? Would buying a water purifier save you $11 a month on bottled water? Looking for companies that consolidate debts—how much stress and cash could you save? Where can you find free money:

1.
2.
3.
4.
5.
6.
7.
8.
9.
10.
11.
12.

A penny saved is a penny earned and is still just a penny, but increases in wealth are not just about money. The stress reduction, removal of distractions, and the ease you have can greatly increase the joy in your household.

Some clip coupons for things they don't normally use, others focus only on what they need. Some see a sale and buy, buy, buy, but others only stock up on necessary items when they're on sale. By buying in bulk, choosing quality over quaintly, and sticking only to what I'll use, I easily find a thousand a year in free money.

But let's return to the idea of solving our debts. On a separate piece of paper, write a list of your debts. It doesn't sound fun, but make one anyway, then read on.

Now, rewrite the debt list, dividing it into two categories on separate pieces of paper: one personal (family and friends) and one cooperate (all others). On each list, arrange the debts from smallest to largest. Then, next to each debt, write the minimum payment required to avoid fines, the interest rate, your account number, and their phone number. Next, call the places you owe and see if there is anything you can do to reduce your interest or minimum payments without acquiring additional debt. Be sure to record the date of each call. For those that did not help, plan to call again in three months, and again three months later. Policies change, and consistent payments may improve your chances.

"Success is not final;
failure is not fatal:
it is the courage to continue that counts."
-Winston Churchill

If you owe money to family and friends (even though they are unlikely to charge you interest), pay them first. Good relations are more important, and they likely need the money as well. Few do this, but if you do not want to be seen as a villain by those closest to you, make this a priority.

Once you've paid back family and friends, begin paying the minimum on all other debts. Use any extra funds to pay off the smallest debt first. Once it is paid, cross it off the list. Then, use the money that was going toward that debt and apply it to the next smallest debt until it, too, is paid off. Seeing this progress and momentum will motivate you to continue with this honorable choice.

If your debt is overwhelming, consider reaching out to a local debt consolidator or lender. They may be able to combine a few of your highest-interest debts into a single loan with payments at half or less of the interest you're currently paying. They may even offer a few months of interest-free savings.

While some aim for the highest interest debt first, seeing progress is more encouraging. When you look at your sheet and see three names and two companies crossed off, you'll feel a sense of accomplishment. Plus, the plan is not just pay, pay, and pay. The calls and consolidation strategy can help reduce many of these debts.

No new debts! Do not add to your lists! Nor leave payments on debts to chance or rely on leftovers at the end of the month. Put 20%-25% of your earnings, as well as any extra from the end of the month, towards debts.

"Many of life's failure are people who did not realize how close they were to success when they gave up."
-Thomas Edison

While paying off debts feels good and seems wise, without the habit of saving money, you will never be debt-free. Paying yourself first provides a cushion in your account, preventing overdraft fees and more debt when unexpected expenses arise—and they always do.

Figure up the total amount you have earned from the time you started working all those years ago to today. It can be a rough estimate, but then take 10% of that number and write it here:

$_____

Wouldn't you feel more comfortable and secure with that in the bank right now? You can still, no matter your age, work toward a higher number. Start today. Go to your bank tomorrow, open a savings account, and begin paying yourself first. But why wait that long, when tomorrow often turns into never? Start today!

Some locked in their interest rates at banks more than 50 years ago and are still getting a 5% return on their money, while others have a savings account that earns just 0.0024% interest. Many argue that CDs, bonds, and savings accounts can't keep up with the cost of living, but not everyone is ready or willing to invest. Even so, a little return is better than none, and not all savings are the same. Some banks are only online and often offer significantly higher interest rates due to lower overhead costs. Some tiny local banks can beat even that as they do not have advertising expenses. And some major banks will at times offer limited-time deals to attract more customers.

Granted, a low-interest savings account with a few thousand in it may only yield you five or six dollars a year.

You could make more by staying an extra half hour at work once a year or skipping one beer. If you have millions, or even tens of thousands, though, finding the safest and highest interest is worth looking into.

"Your past does not equal your future."
-Tony Robbins

With one million, at 0.0055% interest, you will make $5,500 in interest, or $17,000 at 0.017% interest. It would take around 59 years for the interest you receive to match the initial deposit. But, that said, $17,000 is still better than zero.

There are better methods, but if your money is just sitting there, at least allow it to grow some interest, even if it is only a few bucks a year. If nothing more, it is good training to get yourself in the mindset of financial growth.

You can, in a way, start your own savings account. I once had a large jar where all small bills and change would go. An item for $8.88 would become $10.00, as the $1.12 went into the jar. About a year and a half later, I used it to go on a wonderful, long vacation where I pinched pennies but didn't skip any fun. You do not have to waste money to enjoy life.

Many spend hundreds going out to eat. If they made more money, they would simply go out to eat more often, and at fancier locations. We tend to spend what we have, but we don't spend what we have before taxes are taken out of our checks, so consider paying yourself first no differently. Once it's in your savings, that money is gone, and that's that. Write out everything you have spent money on in the last quarter, and you will likely find at least 10% of your income is leaking away on things that don't bring you any real joy.

When I was little, I wanted to earn quarters so I could play arcade games, and Grandmother would say, "That money is burning a hole in your pocket." As a kid, I thought that was silly, but a common habit of the poor is to let money burn holes in their pockets. They spend it as fast as they get it, as if it had fallen out of their wallet or purse the moment they put it in.

Looking again at that list of what you spent in the last quarter—and the lists we made at the very beginning of this workbook—what are some of the holes in your pocket? Is it going out to eat too often? Or is it drinks, from soda to alcohol, that's damaging your life and pocketbook? Do we honor taxes, as well as unhealthily alleged luxuries, more than the security of our families?

It is possible to save 10% of your income. You are more important than video services and bar tabs. It is imperative to see yourself as at least this valuable for your own emotional health, wouldn't you say?

From my savings account, 80% is untouchable unless there is a true emergency (and even then I do my best to not touch it and, so far, have not had to). The other 20% is for investing, be it in gold, stocks, a house to renovate, or the like—none of which I have done yet, but that is fine. When the time is right for me, I will be prepared. Besides, right now, I am making more through buying and selling, and I thoroughly enjoy the jobs I have. And *that* is wealth.

"In most cases being a good boss means hiring talented people, and then getting out of their way."
-Tina Fey

More On Doubling

$\mathcal{D}$oubling may seem strange at first, but let's consider something simple—something I have done many times. You buy an item and sell it for double. Now, sometimes you can only make 25%, and that's fair enough. But I have bought toys in bulk and sold them for more than triple. It can be done. Every store you go to is already doing this, after all.

Let's say you start with $500. You buy, sell, and make double. You now have $1,000. Many people just say, "Oh, boy!" and buy a bunch of games to waste their time with. But instead, imagine doubling it nine more times:

Doubling $500 = $1,000 = $2,000 = $4,000 = $8,000 = $16,000 = $32,000 = $64,000 = $128,000 = $256,000 = $512,000

One more time and you have over a million.

Granted, you cannot do this. Right?

No one has or can, so you can't either. Right?

Actually, again, every store does this.

When I ran a small health food store, I was utterly shocked at how little the vitamins I take actually cost. All supplements are marked up at least 100%, but many are by 400%! Even if you only mark up by 25%, it does not take long to see a great return.

From selling cars to land, from collectible baseball cards to works of art, some sales can total years' worth of income. But you may need to start small—selling toys, salt and pepper shakers, used books, or coffee presses. Whatever it is, start now and invest in yourself.

Dreaming about, or simply understanding this concept, is pointless. You must **start**.

Cheap Stuff Costs Too Much

Once, after living on a box of *Cream of Wheat* for a week, and after paying my bills, I had $100 left for basic necessities. All my light bulbs were burnt out, I had been using napkins for toilet paper, and I had no soap let alone food. So I bought the cheapest things I could find to replace everything I needed. Walking back home with those large bags, I was so proud of how much I had saved.

But the light bulbs were burnt out before the month was over. The dish and laundry soap smelled awful and were so ineffective that I had to use many times the normal amount. Even with extra rinses and hanging my clothes outside, they stunk worse than my dirty clothes. The food made me feel weak—the white bread had no protein to speak of, the potatoes had green skins and tasted horrible, and everything had less nutritional value than that blasted *Cream of Wheat*! The tool I needed broke before I finished using it. And, to this day, I recall standing in my dark apartment, saying, "I am too poor to afford cheap things."

After another paycheck, I went and bought a small bag of goods. One set of light bulbs were supposed to last 10 years, and another said they would last 15 years. When I picked up the 15-year ones, my cousin said, "What are you doing? Those are too expensive!" I told her the cheap ones cost so much more. Those bulbs lasted me over 20 years. The food I bought was healthier, and this improved my work, thinking ability, and well-being, leading to better pay. The cheap loaf of bread had 1/5 to a 1/10th the value, from protein to minerals, as the slightly more expensive bread. The better loaf also filled me up for less money since I needed less to get the same value. And, this time, the tool not only worked but still works.

Sometimes, I still make the mistake of buying the cheap stuff, but it always, and I mean always, winds up costing me more. I buy a cheap tool, it breaks, and I end up buying a quality tool. I buy a cheap speaker, but the sound is tinny and the volume is low, so I take it back and buy a higher-quality speaker. After all, I will be listening to it for several hours a day for many years. So why not start with quality?

"The bitterness of poor quality remains long after the sweetness of low price is forgotten."
-Benjamin Franklin

That said, I love it when a product I use, or food I eat, is on sale. I do the math and decide how much I normally use, and how long it will last, and then stock up. Say a food item you often eat at work is normally $4.24 but is on sale for $2.99, you could buy enough for three to four months (given its one-year shelf life). That $1.25 savings per item adds up to $100—and you are going to eat it anyway. Saving money does not mean buying cheap items, or things you don't use just because they're on sale. It means buying good stuff you already use when it is on sale.

Again, living frugally doesn't have to mean surviving on cheap ramen. It could mean cooking lentils and rice with greens and fruits from your garden. So be it. Even adventure doesn't have to be determined by high or low price points. Instead of an overseas flight, it could be exploring local parks, museums, or libraries and finding ways to enjoy life without excessive spending.

If you had no choice but to live on half of your current income, you would find ways to do it. For the price of one goody, you could buy four bags of beans. For what it costs in time to go and buy greens, you could harvest them yourself. If you own a large freezer, visit people who have fruit trees and ask if you could harvest some. No one has told me no, and if they ever do, no problem. I have had my freezer filled with frozen apples, raspberries, blueberries, bananas, and the like from free sources. Maybe I would like fresh blackberries from the store, but using the fruit I have in my shakes is free. How could you use this mindset to have good stuff for less?

"The most important thing to do if you find yourself in a hole is to stop digging."
-Warren Buffett

Avoiding Scams

From telemarketers to partnerships with a brother, there are many scams out there, some of which do not appear as such. Explaining how to avoid them completely isn't possible, but two truths tie for the best advice: Only engage in honest dealings, and never put yourself in a position where, if something fails, it crushes you.

Cliché perhaps, but when things sound too good to be true, they usually are. The lottery tells you how you could win, yet the chances are one in tens of millions. We hear about how to use an advertising deal to reach more people, but then discover that instead of reaching a hundred thousand people, it was just trashy spam and now the company's name is tarnished. It lost customers!

When a site has a pop-up, I leave it. When there are more ads than content, I leave. When the deal only lasts a few hours, forget it. Avoiding scams takes practice and awareness. Are you only buying that food item because you have a coupon? Are there loopholes in a contract with your business partner? Has it been evaluated by professionals?

Getting conned happens to us all; there is no reason to feel shame or even blame mixed with unforgiveness when you've been wronged. From phony emails to giving your information to an untrustworthy site, we've all fallen for something. We've all probably also used manipulation to get someone to help, make a sale, avoid a bill, or pass a test.

Using foresight, ask: "While perfect now, what happens if my partner (business or even marriage) ruins this company or union? What can I do to protect myself while still being honorable—even in the eyes of my competitors and in-laws?"

To avoid scams, we have to train ourselves to recognize them. Right now, I want you to find 10 scams in your home and business. I'll give you an example. I recently purchased a supplement to try out. Often the container is twice as big as needed just to get you to buy it—such a huge waste that winds up in landfills! Yet, this one really took it to a new level. That jar was 10 times bigger than needed for those little pills. And not only that, I was supposed to take two of the tiny things, making it half of what I thought I was getting. There was no reason to not put the full dose in one pill (it still would have been tiny). This was a scam, and I fell for it.

Where are the scams hiding in your home or company? Search for them to learn how to avoid being taken advantage of, and to cease employing dishonesty yourself.

1.
2.
3.
4.
5.
6.
7.
8.
9.
10.

Five Rules of Acquisition from the Ferengi Empire:
3: Never spend more for an acquisition than you have to.
8: Small print leads to large risk.
34: War is good for business.
35: Peace is good for business.
217: Always know what you're buying.

Physical Rejuvenation

Nutrient saturation enhances cognitive and physical performance, directly increasing wealth. Without a healthy body, what good would millions or billions of dollars be? No one would accept millions of dollars if they had to suffer and die from lung cancer for the next few months—yet some pay to do it through smoking cigarettes. Unhealthy people will pay everything they have and go into debt for life—but not to get healthy, no, just to survive. And yet, they cringe when told to spend a few extra dollars on higher-quality food so they can thrive.

Madness—if there ever was! That is true madness.

Clichés abound about how this is the only body you'll ever have, but to have true wealth, you must prioritize health. Not just healthier and stronger—you can actually become younger! In many ways, we can reverse aging and repair the damage of life. This is so important that it is worth a whole workbook. If you have not read *Hero, Vol. 2*, do so. If you have read it, but are not yet applying it, put this workbook down for now. Without health, no amount of money can buy you wealth.

"Work never killed anyone.
It's worry that does the damage.
And the worry would disappear
if we'd just settle down and do the work."
-Earl Nightingale

Setting Your House In Order

When I was 30, I looked at charts showing how much fairly secure investments could grow if started at 20 instead of 30. It was so disheartening that I just didn't bother, which, of course, was stupid.

What do you have to provide income when you can no longer work? What *if* social security fails? Like creating streams of income, preparing for old age is something you must actively work towards, rather than hope it just magically takes care of itself.

From stocks to bonds, from savings accounts to 401(k)s and Roth IRAs, the sooner you start saving, the better. The differences in returns between starting at 20 versus 40 are staggering. For those with wise parents, who start these things for them as infants—those kids will retire with abundance.

"Set your house in perfect order
before you criticize the world."
-Dr. Jordan Peterson

But not everyone lives to retirement, and one out of one of us will die.

In preparation, it is helpful if there is very little rubbish in your home. Not only does this provide a better living situation for yourself, but it also makes life easier for loved ones after you're gone. Instead of leaving boxes of old receipts, broken keepsakes, and worn-out clothes, make sure that at least 95% of what you own is something others would value. The junk drawer that is now twelve boxes? No one wants that. They also don't want stress. Sometimes what people saved gets taken by courts and villains. Our diligence in this is an essential aspect of wealth management. Without proper documentation, your bank can't just give your money to your best friend or a charity. In this, it is imperative to have everything in order. No matter your age or income, make sure you have the following:

- A Last Will with an audio recording sharing thoughts with loved ones
- Medical and financial POAs
- A Roth IRA
- A 401(k)
- Investments in companies you support, not just those you think will grow
- Clear instructions with your bank regarding beneficiaries
- Savings and business accounts
- A credit card offering high cash-back rewards
- An accountant to help reduce taxes legally
- Life insurance with designated primary and contingent beneficiaries
- A fireproof, heatproof, waterproof, and secure safe containing all titles, financial summaries, passwords, PINs, Will, and your final wishes—or even a pre-arranged and paid-for cremation or plan for natural burial

Now, when you pass away, your loved ones have the least amount of work possible to do.

We often think we'll handle these tasks when we're older, but many of us don't reach old age—or lose the ability to address these issues by then. So, whether you're 18 or 80, start today. Regularly review your preparations and ask: What's one more thing I can do to make this process easier for people to take care of?

Setting your house in order means handling both life and death matters. So, do not overlook the little things. Much of our pain—from legal trouble to job loss—stems from poorly handled emotions. And part of our lack of control comes from having too many little problems in our lives.

"Do not save what is left after spending,
but spend what is left after saving."
-Warren Buffett

Each of your small problems may not seem like much individually, but, when combined, they weaken your ability to handle life. Unlike large difficulties, it is hard to pinpoint these kinds of issues because they are scattered and seemingly insignificant. Think of little things left undone as if they are weights piled upon you. Sure, the garden pots that have been sitting alongside the house for three years only weigh half a pound, and the door that sticks, the junk mail you get every day, and the cans of soup you don't like—well, all those may only add up to two pounds. Many people's jacket weighs more than all that! Right? But add another forty, fifty, or a hundred things to that, and you could be burdened down all day every day without knowing why.

"He who buys what he does not need,
steals from himself."
-Swedish Proverb

Some suggest starting with a list, but I've found a list can be daunting to make or even look at. Instead, take a few moments every day and attack a little thing in your life. And here is the fun part, though it may not sound like it at first:

write those little things down right after you do them. Why? Within a week, you can look back at a whole slew of tiny annoyances that are now gone.

Imagine if your list looked like this:

- The junk drawer is clean
- Messy papers are no longer on the stand
- Cleaned a corner for all the garden tools
- Removed the bumper sticker from my car
- Took down the broken doorbell
- Gave Tom back his books

It may not seem like much, but even these small victories can give you quite a sigh of relief, as well as the desire to do a little thing tomorrow—or even right now.

What three places do you spend the most time in? Is it your bed, garage, and station at work? If each of these areas were clean and had no nagging unfinished projects, would you have less stress in your life? When was the last time you cleaned out your pantry and refrigerator? If you collected all the food you do not want to keep, where could you take it so people in need could benefit? And what could you do to prevent future food waste?

What projects could you let go of today? Do not feel as though you have failed by letting them go; instead, think of it as freeing yourself so other projects can succeed. You can also decide not to take on more projects, which is another way to set your house in order. Those victories should also be added to your list of small successes.

But life is not just about your goals. What little project or stressor of a loved one's could you help with? Does your wife dislike the dirty window she looks through all day? Does your son feel annoyed at how something is positioned? And (yeah, I mean it) does your dog or cat fear that odd plastic glittery thing you brought back from some random party? Then get rid of it. It is surprising how much our loved one's pain or stress can become our own. But do not take this step for gain. Do it because you care.

> *"The price of anything*
> *is the amount of life you exchange for it."*
> *-Henry David Thoreau*

The act of looking for missing things, from tools to keys, causes billions in lost revenue every year. We fail to see how much a cluttered home, unpaid bills, or even small apologies left unsaid, can build up in our lives, robbing ourselves and our loved ones of peace, safety, and happiness.

But, like all these steps, it will not work unless you do. So, right now, before reading on, accomplish one little thing to set your house in order, and then write it down. Tomorrow, do another thing and record it. In thirty days, your life will have improved greatly. The first thing many write on that list? 1. Bought a high-quality safe for important documents.

> *"A designer knows he has achieved perfection*
> *not when there is nothing left to add,*
> *but when there is nothing left to take away."*
> *-Antoine De Saint-Exupéry*

Minimalism & Maximization

*E*xtended traveling teaches us this simple truth: we need far less than we think. We get annoyed when we lug around X, Y, and Z but never use those items. Even when packing our clothes, we only choose our best and favorites. We do not pack a collection of trinkets and knickknacks, let alone boxes of junk we keep around just in case. In reality, living a rich life requires surprisingly little. Our daily essentials don't demand a huge house or storage shed to contain them. In this, minimalism and maximization are essentially the same. We can only be minimal if what we own adds maximum value to our lives.

> *"Edit your life frequently and ruthlessly.*
> *It's your masterpiece, after all."*
> *-Nathan W. Morris*

Have you sold money for poverty? Is what you enjoy buried in the clutter of gizmos and junk? Most of us own things we do not truly want, and are thereby owned by those items! Look at what you buy, buy into, or collect (even if you are not a collector), and apply the following steps.

The basics of minimalism and maximization is to look at an item and ask these three questions:

1. Do I use it often?
2. Is it beautiful?
3. Is it the best?

Then:

1. Place frequently used items in the most accessible spots. If you use it weekly or less, store it out of sight. If you rarely or never use it, there is no need to keep it.

2. If an item is useful but not beautiful, store it neatly out of sight.

3. When evaluating if something is the best or not, remember that newer doesn't always mean better. However, if something is flimsy, broken, or does a poor job, it's worth considering a replacement.

"Perhaps you are overvaluing what you don't have
and undervaluing what you do."
-Dr. Jordan Peterson

Example: While your tape gun works, you've cut yourself with it before, often cuss while using it due to its flimsy design, and only use it a few times a month even though it always sits on the edge of your desk.

Do you use it often? No. Is it beautiful? No. Is it the best? Most assuredly not! So:

1. Find a high-quality tape gun and replace it. After clearing the rubbish and unused items out of a desk drawer, place the new, quality tape gun inside. This space will now be more pleasant. You have a useable tool that you enjoy rather than cuss at, and there is less ugly clutter sitting where you are supposed to be creative. Now, when you open that drawer, there will only be enjoyable tools you use on occasion. If you never use the tape gun or other item, don't replace it. And if you need one next year, borrow one from a shipping office.

"It is right to be content with what we have,
but never with what we are."
-Sir James Mackintosh

2. As silly as it may sound, I was advised to follow this simple ritual when getting rid of an item: Pick up the item, say, 'Thank you' to it, and place it gently in the trash, recycling bin, or a box to donate or sell." Somehow, this gratitude helps.

3. Reinforce the decision by enjoying the space and keeping it clean and organized. Work created at a cluttered desk will never be as inspiring or beautiful as work created in an atmosphere of tranquility. While classical music playing, a good writing tool, proper lighting, and works of art on the wall are by no means required (you can write in prison, after all), having an organized space will be much more inspiring. Limit things to what is **useful**, **inspiring**, and **functional**. This is an opportunity for emotional growth and maturity by detaching ourselves from mere things.

"He who is not contented with what he has,
would not be contented with what he would like to have."
-Socrates

The goal is not a house with less. It is a home filled with function and beauty. A well-organized home or room allows other areas of life to flourish. Instead of falling prey to greed, gluttony, and consumerism, letting go of the weight of unnecessary stress will free up emotional energy for other areas of your life. If we apply these concepts, our lives, and the lives of those around us, will improve.

Take a moment to picture your entire house this way. Then take another moment to clean a small area today. Another tiny space can be done tomorrow, creating another line of success. It does not take long and can be fun if you allow it to be—the practice of minimalism and maximization.

"A big group of daily friends or a white painted house with
bills and mirrors, are not a necessity to me
— but an intelligent conversation
while sharing another coffee, is."
-Charlotte Eriksson

Exclusions:

1. Keepsakes. Only part with them if they can be gifted to someone who will treasure them.

2. Shared belongings. If someone in your household isn't ready to let go of an item, respect their decision. Make sure this process is fun for everyone and is done for only a few minutes per day.

Example: Let's say you have Jim's old pocket watch. You liked the man, but it just sits there.

1. You know Jim and your cousin Mary were close, so you give that watch to her. Now, rather than a watch that does not work in a box you seldom go through, you have a memory of Mary's eyes filled with happiness and tears. That is a greater wealth than hanging onto Jim's old watch, just because you thought you were supposed to.

I did this once with two old plates. One had a little town's church on it, and the other had a tiny motel from the same town. With quite a bit of effort, I found the people who once owned the motel and gave them the plate. They were overcome with joy. Unbeknownst to me, a fire had destroyed their keepsakes of what had been their passion and livelihood for decades. That memory is worth far more than the ten bucks I could have sold it for. And the church plate now hangs in the preacher's office. From handbags to blankets, from paintings to tools, sometimes the best way to preserve a keepsake is through the joy your gifts bring to others.

2. This is difficult if someone wants to keep everything. One way to help is by trading. Three random paintings for a truly cherished one. Two dented pans for a quality one. Three so-so books for an exceptional one.

Maximization is rarely spoken of. One of the greatest investments I've made is in the place where I spend 8 hours of my life every day: a high-quality bed—and even more so, a pillow I enjoy. This computer with a non-glare screen has also been a pleasant upgrade. What can you do to improve your home, ranging from your toolbox to kitchen pantry?

Subtracting to add and adding to multiply is the subtle art of minimalism and maximization. If you take your time and have fun with it, this will enhance your life and household.

Once you have done this, do it again. Look at each thing you own and ask, "Would I pay double its worth to keep it?" If not, sell it. If a book isn't worth reading twice, then it isn't worth reading once. Or say an item broke, would you replace it? If the painting on your wall were ruined, would you spend double to replace it? If not, get rid of it. That is not art, it's clutter. Are you listening to music you would not be excited to see live? If not, it is not music—it's background noise.

Continue by looking in places you either rarely think about or actively avoid. Do you need all that makeup? Are you sure? What about all those blocks of wood in the garage? Or those three meetings this week—do you have to be there, or could a couple be dropped?

Replacing negative habits with intentional ones is another form of decluttering. Remove the morning news filled with negativity and replace it with a rule: only positive things can be said during breakfast. You do not need the news, at least not much of it. But you do need friends, family, and emotional well-being. Keep and increase those.

Another way to declutter is through prevention. Ask yourself, "In a year, is this going to be on my list of things to get rid of?" Or, "If I need it right now, but never again, can I borrow this item instead?"

What belongings of yours are emotional purchases? Food? Clothing? What are steps you can take to avoid buying when overly emotional?

"Your home is living space, not storage space."
-Francine Jay

Walking into a room with a mesmerizing painting, a clean desk, an elegant chair, and a stand with a cactus, as opposed to a room with 348 things all over the place, brings about peace, inspiration, and tranquility.

Clutter keeps you in the past, emboldens procrastination, and breeds confusion, which manifests as anxiety and depression, and these, in turn, can manifest as anger.

By removing everything that does not serve a function in that room—well, are you setting your house in order or are you cleaning your character and mindset? The answer to both is yes. Your dwelling is an extension of your character, and the more you refine it, the more you draft your hero. No hero lives in a messy, dismal dwelling, but villains do.

Grant yourself the ability to pursue a meaningful life through responsibility and the pursuit of passions rather than possessions. From addressing the not-really-wanted things cluttering your room as much as your mind, to helping your partner finish their project, these steps to wealth will help free you of a little nagging voice you never knew you had.

Another minimal thing? My quarterly newsletter. (Most of us subscribe to too many of those, too—but four times a year is pretty comfy). It isn't much. Just a free mini e-book, updates on future books, and some fun surprises. If that sounds fair, go to www.emotionalmanagement.org to sign up.

"If you cannot afford yourself any luxuries for the time being, at least offer yourself the one priceless luxury no one can take away from you—your time"
-Lauren Klarfeld

Don't Weaken

Warren Buffett once said the first rule is to not lose money, and the second rule is to remember the first rule. Even if we have windfalls, be it from unexpected events or bigger wins in business, if we lose ground the rest of the time, we haven't truly gained anything. It's like someone going to the gym and having an epic workout, only to eat and sleep poorly for the next three months. Better a mild, consistent workout paired with quality food and sleep, and then repeat it the next day. Don't lose wealth.

The richest people I've met drive cheap, used vehicles and live in modest homes. Many of the poorest people I know have expensive, brand-new cars and renovated houses—but they are in debt for the next 30 years or more! Due to paying interest, their house costs two or three times as much, and their new car lost 30+% of its value the moment they drove it off the lot! Don't lose money.

If you buy a car or house—or even an outfit or piece of gym equipment—ask yourself, "If I decide to sell this tomorrow, will I be able to get the same amount or more than I paid for it?" If the answer is no, then adhere to rule number two and look to rule number one. Don't lose money. Ignoring this will cost you wealth.

*"I always tried to turn every disaster
into an opportunity."*
-John D. Rockefeller

Do I Need This Today In Order To Live?

This is a difficult habit to develop because we often want goodies rather than what is good. But every time you pick up anything to buy for yourself, ask, "Do I need this today in order to live?" If the answer is no, then do not buy it. Of course, this requires common sense—buy groceries and pay for necessities like gas or insurance, especially if paying in full earns you a discount in money or time. But do you need that fizzy drink, chocolate bar, or pricey pre-made meal?

Start by knowing your weekly grocery budget, and then spend less than that. The only way to stay out of debt or get ahead is to spend less than you make. Do that and you will never be broke. But even if you have thousands to spend on food, that does not mean you should spend it all. That is where everyone goes wrong. What if you could only spend $100 this week on food, and that food had to be the healthiest options possible? What would you get?

Do not be taken in by advertisements for new fashions or foods. Finding a handmade no-name-brand article of clothing that you like should always mean more to you than a name-brand. And when was the last time you saw ads for carrots or celery? We never will. The sick care system of America (and the world) would collapse if we all took care of our health.

"Eyes blinded by the fog of things cannot see truth.
Ears deafened by the din of things cannot hear truth.
Brains bewildered by the whirl of things cannot think truth.
Hearts deadened by the weight of things cannot feel truth.
Throats choked by the dust of things cannot speak truth."
-Harold Bell Wright

Golden Touch

When I was a kid, I played a game where everything I touched with my pinky turned into the gold it was worth. I had to be careful to not turn myself into gold, and—*oh no, I touched the dog!* Truth is, I sometimes play this as an adult, too, where everything I touch turns into the money I spent on it. The game always ends with me realizing how few things I actually want.

While you can do this by selling items or, better yet, not buying them to begin with, the golden touch I have in mind is much more enriching than these.

There are three types of touches:

1. What you touch can turn to ruin.

You read a book on happiness, and it becomes poison through mockery. You touch a tree, and it dies from neglect. A waiter forgets about you, brings the wrong order, doesn't refill your water, and never brings the bill.

Your experience is unpleasant.

2. What you touch can stay the same.

You touch a book on happiness, but it remains a book for other people. You touch a tree, and, while watered, it still needs to be properly pruned. The waiter delivers your food, filled your water, and brings your bill.

Standard at best.

Midas wished everything he touched would turn into gold.
He thought his greed would enrich him beyond
his most fanciful dreams. But when touching his
daughter to comfort her woes, she turned from
an invaluable woman into meaningless gold.

3. What you touch can turn to gold.

A book on happiness transforms your life, and the lives of those around you, forever. A tree, eloquently pruned, bears fruit, and people stop to admire it. The server goes above and beyond, engaging in lively conversation, clearing dishes promptly, and creating an atmosphere so inviting that it feels like this is your restaurant. He even sends tea home for your mother and helped carry your bags to the car.

This is golden.

From businesses to marriages, we have the power to turn them to ruin, let them stay the same, or turn them into gold.

How many restaurants out of a thousand could be better? The obvious answer: one thousand.

How many people could become healthier and fitter? 99% seems like a low estimate.

How many could improve their marriage? Obviously, the answer is every couple.

Ah, but how many think they can—let alone should— improve their income? Most believe only 1% can, and that they aren't in that 1%—even though every rags-to-riches story disproves it. Yet, we seldom hear of middle-class-to-riches. Why? While they're not wholly comfortable, they are comfortable enough to not pursue wealth any further. In the richest places and times, you will find those living in poverty, inasmuch as you will find wealthy people in the poorest places. Wealth is *not* situational.

Say someone's wife asks him to make her a cup of tea. The touch of ruin would be to use a used tea bag, bring stale coffee instead, or even just refuse. The touch of common would be plain tea in a glass. The golden touch, however, requires more than merely bringing her favorite tea—the husband must research how to brew that tea to perfection. He watched her place a touch of sugar in her glass, and so he also adds some. Instead of a plain cup, he brings it in her favorite cup, which he had to wash. Add to it a saucer, a kiss, a brief neck massage, another kiss, and a smile—and he does it all without even being asked because he knows she loves tea when she reads. That is golden! _That_ is wealth.

"It's no accident that most ads are pitched to people in their 20s and 30s. Not only are they so much cuter than their elders ... but they are less likely to have gone through the transformative process of cleaning out their deceased parents' stuff. Once you go through that, you can never look at 'your' stuff in the same way. You start to look at your stuff a little postmortemistically. If you've lived more than two decades as an adult consumer, you probably have quite the accumulation, even if you're not a hoarder ... I'm not saying I never buy stuff, because I absolutely do. Maybe I'm less naive about the joys of accumulation."
-Roz Chast

You cannot fake this, but you can grow incrementally. Everyone can. Start by caring as much as you can. Then, in time, care a little more, making it enjoyable for all. Then, care a little more. That's how you turn yourself into gold. That's how you create real wealth.

Think of the woman drinking tea above. What if she were rich but not wealthy? Her tea might be brought to her by a servant as she sat in a fancy home, while her husband barely noticed her. She might not even look up to see if he was there. Despite their millions, they are poverty-stricken.

Most of us would rather go to a restaurant where the cook and waitress are fun but the food is just okay than one with great food but has employees who are jerks because they hate being there. I have watched businesses go under for the sole reason that the employees were unhappy. Kindness is a cornerstone of real wealth—in your pocketbook and heart.

It does go both ways, though. Employees get enough rotten customers. To have a golden touch, we must enhance our heroic superpower of empathy—caring for our caregivers is essential for a healthier world.

Take a gas station for another example. They used to have men come out and fill up your car, all while washing your windows, checking your oil, tires, and lights, and telling you the news or clean jokes. Maybe that would be cost-inhibitive, but consider a smaller step, such as offering free candy inside to every customer or placing up a sign letting people know assistance is available. These small gestures could attract customers who might end up buying more—or at the very least, leave thinking, "What a nice place. They checked our car, and it was low on oil. We had no idea. And they gave us a goodie, and were honestly friendly."

As for me, while I have mentioned them before, I always go to the same auto shop. The ladies there are not only good mechanics but are enjoyable to speak with, remember my name, and share stories while I am there. Granted, I also bring them goodies sometimes from the farmers' market, ranging from baked goods to flowers, and I took time to learn their names. Indeed, being a hero goes both ways, but someone has to start the kindness, and it may as well be us.

"It takes as much energy to wish as it does to plan."
-Eleanor Roosevelt

Focus & Comfort

The term "priorities" is silly since you can only have one priority, and that one priority is to do one thing every day to reach your goal—not just busy work or research. Some of the best lessons come from doing the work, even if poorly at first. In fact, poorly is inevitable. Don't chase perfectionism. It is the lowest aim because it is not achievable.

Focus-producing advancement is interrupted most of all by comfort. Allow yourself to be miserable about where you are now. Comfortable cats, people, and dogs tend to not move or change their environment, and it need only be comfortable enough. By spending money on luxuries, you make living in misery more comfortable and thus stay there.

If you removed all unnecessary things from your life, would you still be happy where you are? If you had no videos or games, no slippers or comfortable reclining chairs, would you still be happy? The difference between the middle class and lower class is one has more luxuries in their discomfort. True poverty is not a lack of money, but a lack of worth. If you are worth a low wage, you'll always be poor, even if you win the lottery. If you supply the value of a thousandfold, you will be rich, even if living in squalor. The secret of being rich is to be valuable; the secret of staying that way is to live humbly; and the secret to finding happiness in wealth is being present and giving. Individual people have helped charities more than whole towns do. Do not just daydream about the results; learn to fantasize about the process as well.

"If you could only love enough,
you could be the most powerful person in the world."
-Emmet Fox

180

Discovering New Passions

Find a dozen rare and extraordinarily fun niches within your passions. Not writing for a newspaper, as that is vague and not strange enough. Which paper, and what subjects?

Still don't know what to do? Instead of looking at your joys, try looking at your curses. Consider a man who has struggled horrifically with alcoholism—lost family, spent time in prison, battled it and failed for decades—and yet has fought it and won. Maybe, as a consequence of writing a book on it, his battle becomes a heroic tale with purpose. From obese to healthy, from violent to peaceful, these people help us see a path that works. Trauma, however, is not a requirement. The woman who never drank or who has always been healthy and fit also has a story to tell—we could learn so much from those who have not gone down dark paths of addiction and self-harm.

And sometimes curses are strange. I knew a woman who looked like she was 12—or maybe only 10. Her real age? 35. There are groups who train women like her to infiltrate child prostitution rings so they can arrest these criminals. From finding one man trying to buy sex from a child to taking down dozens of locations where children are kept as slaves, this woman, who once thought her appearance was a curse, now sees it as a blessing to others and herself.

Look to where your passions draw you, obviously, but also look to struggles, triumphs won with or without a battle, and at the uniqueness of you.

"We are not limited by our old age;
we are liberated by it."
-Stu Mittleman

Referrals

Sometimes a client only earns you a few hundred a year, but she tells so many people about you that all her referrals earn you tens of thousands. Other clients may earn you a few thousand a year, but they cause the most stress, loss of time, and give you no referrals. Many trip over themselves to be nice to customers who don't care but ignore customers who keep them in business just through their referrals alone.

Some offer discounts on your next order if you can prove you told friends, but this seems a little shady to me. It might be better to say something like, "Bring a friend, and they get in for free." Or, "If this helped you, it could help others. Please post this or share it." Or even, "If you are a fan of our music and kindness, then your kindness would be music to our hearts. Tell your friends about us. Thanks love!"

To further encourage referrals, provide value that your customer never knew was part of the deal. This needn't be huge. From a free ebook to an after-dinner mint, from a taster at a brewery to scraps for your dog from a restaurant, providing camaraderie is important. If a manual is necessary, that should be part of the package, but consider adding a fun bonus too. A cool keychain, hat, or phone cover when someone buys your mower, car cover, or decal set is not only an unexpected treat for them but also a way for them to remember you, spread the word, or buy again. And above-average experience will always encourage referrals.

"Business is the art of extracting money from another man's pocket without resorting to violence."
-Max Amsterdam

Test Your Product

Have you ever bought something—from clothing to food, from a tool to a toy—and paused to wonder, "Did these people ever use their product?" I have boxers where the top always rolls down and the inside seams are somehow sharp. Did the people who made these ever wear a pair? What about packages that are nearly impossible to get open—is this intentional? Are they deriving some perverse satisfaction out of this? People who make cars should be rewarded for their labor, as well as have to work on those cars for a few years. If the designers had to become the mechanics, cars would be much easier to work on.

Rant aside, test your product. From restaurants where the prongs on the fork are sharp like needles to items that get damaged just by being opened, or wasteful packaging that's five times bigger than necessary—test your products.

And editors are not just for authors! How many times have you laughed at the poor grammar in instructions? Make sure your customers easily understand and enjoy your written materials. Mistakes are going to occur, but, by minimizing them, we retain customers' appreciation. If you ever sell internationally, hire a professional editor who is a native speaker to look over your message—even if only a sentence!

"Try not to become a man of success
but rather try to become a man of value."
-Albert Einstein

Is There More?

Shine a light on one thing, and more are illumined. As you grow your wealth, explore new ways to enhance and enjoy life with loved ones.

The best three strategies for this are:
1. Start by applying what you know.
2. Record your methods.
3. Ask the best questions you can.

Start by applying what you know:
Wisdom unapplied is willing stupidity. From business to marriage, if you are not growing, you are dying. There is no such thing as standing still. You either progress or regress.

Work on your methods to gain followers, improve your business, begin a side job, and excel at your current work. Stick to this, working on it each day, for at least a year. Decide quickly, and adapt slowly if necessary. Compare this to not starting at all, or deciding slowly and changing so often that you never see if an idea will work. It is clear which approach leads to success—or even the chance of success.

"Even if you are on the right track,
you'll get run over if you just sit there."
-Will Rodgers

Record your methods:
As mentioned earlier in this workbook, write and refine a personal teacher's manual for your passion, business, and

relationships. Write and repeatedly refine what you've written and you will refine your passions, relationships, and yourself.

Some cooks go home exhausted.

Some cooks go home smiling.

Those who work hard in real estate make money.

But those who love working in real estate build wealth.

Success and failure can happen whether doing what you hate or love. When you fail to achieve success while doing what you like, you may not even notice, as passions are enjoyable struggles. If you love what you do, then the idea of writing down methods and lessons to enhance your craft will be exciting—even if you do not enjoy writing. Regardless, we need adversity to overcome. So we will either find it in passion and work, or we will create drama that isn't real. The choice is yours.

"Don't mistake activity with achievement."
-John Wooden

Ask the best questions you can:

The best questions (asked of the right people) provide unfathomable results. Poor questions, on the other hand, give you poor answers. Some examples of good questions:

What one step could reduce or remove other steps?

A new lens does not make beautiful photographs (a good eye does), but what tools would improve my passion?

How can my business plan account for unforeseen injury, pregnancy, or a passing?

Am I so invaluable to the company that it could never sell without me also selling myself?

Since I have to go to work and school on time, what are my self-employed hours?

Who do my mentors recommend I seek advice from?

How can I take responsibility to improve myself past the handicaps of myself and my environment?

How can I make every transaction 100% honorable?

Once you start asking these questions, something peculiar begins to happen. It is called intuition. When you sense that X is unsafe, or that you should keep doing Y but stop doing Z, even if you do not understand why, listen to that inner voice. If you do, that voice will grow stronger. If you don't, it will fade until it becomes silent.

What is intuition? I have no idea. Some say it is your smarter subconscious; others believe it is a spirit—yours or another's—but whatever it is, listen. Follow your heart, your gut, and your intuition in life and business. And if you hone this instinct, you'll see your natural talents, passions, and life's purpose not just for what they are, but for what they could become.

From space travel to surgery, fantasy stories to classic songs, the minds of people have created uncountable wonders. If you use your mind, and value it enough to care for the health thereof, you, too, can bring your passions to life. From practicing visualization each morning and right before sleep to repeatedly reading great books until you know them as well as the author, there are countless ways to build the confidence to move towards wealth.

"Rather than love,
than money,
than fame,
give me truth."
-Henry David Thoreau

Beyond Money

True wealth should be aimed at, as well as enjoyed and celebrated along the way, otherwise, what is the point?

Writing resolutions is often frowned upon, as they are seldom kept and are, frankly, boring. However, writing things out is crucial for achieving our wealth goals in all areas of life. If we do not write down what we are aiming for, as well as what we have achieved, we miss out on fully experiencing the joy of our progress.

In this, writing resolutions needs to become joyful. Do not treat the next section like a task, but a privilege granted to you by birthright.

Making resolutions on a monthly basis is much more effective than on a yearly basis, as we are always growing into new versions of ourselves who set more refined and higher goals than we once had. Rather than cracking the whip or pushing towards a goal that no longer inspires you, monthly goals can be achieved, seen, and celebrated.

Most resolutions revolve around stopping bad habits like smoking or losing fat, but what if we aimed towards, not shame or money, but worth and wealth? Having joy is wealth! So even if you are like my brother who hates making New Year's resolutions (he makes the same one every year: "I'm not going to swallow any whole watermelons."), give this unorthodox method a try.

"I am thankful for all of those who said no to me.
It's because of them, I'm doing it myself."
-Albert Einstein

Resolutions

The components of an enjoyable life are:

Love
Health
Meaning
Wealth
Happiness

I could also add faith, but I would equate this with meaning. While, again, most resolutions are about fat, smoking, money—surface-level goals—these deeper values bring far greater richness to life.

Beginnings are powerful times to set goals, but few keep New Year's resolutions past the end of February. Gyms are packed in January since the most common resolution is weight loss, but empty by March since time dulls our initial motivation and the reasoning is flawed. Many say they want to "lose weight," but if you lose 10 pounds of fat and gain 10 pounds of muscle, the result will not budge a scale. Pursuing goals from a place of self-love and enjoyment makes continuous improvement sustainable while being driven by shame weakens us. So, what if instead of relying on worn-out traditions, you create your own roadmap to wealth and joy—one that changes with you? And what if you design systems, not before the journey begins, but as you travel?

"You can get excited about the future.
The past won't mind."
-Hillary DePiano

Festival: Have a celebration to mark the end of each month, not with destructive behavior, but with intentional joy. One month, that may be enjoying great food or seeing a film. The next month, you may choose to sit in meditation and light incense or go camping in the woods alone or with friends. But each is a celebration to commemorate the passing of the old and the beginning of new opportunities for success. Every month, you get to write a new chapter!

Theme: At the end of each month, choose a different theme, such as Joy or Clearance. Let it be fun, yet have meaning to you. We cannot know exactly where we'll want to be in five years since we will not be the same person then, so a general idea rooted in heart is sufficient guidance.

"Write it on your heart that every day
is the best day in the year."
-Ralph Waldo Emerson

Goals: Eating healthier or spending less can be measured in a gram or a penny. What are you looking forward to doing (not just accomplishing), for Love, Health, Meaning, Wealth, and Happiness? Write out copies of the two New Month Festival pages in a plain notebook, or print them from www.emotionalmanagement.org and make resolutions based on joy, not guilt, on gain, not loss. Keep them simple enough to complete, yet exciting and important enough that interruptions won't derail you. A key to success is to let your work become more enjoyable than time off!

Rewards: Make sure your rewards are true rewards. Do not eat a pound cake for losing a pound. Instead, regardless of whether you lost the weight, if you kept your resolutions this week, treat yourself to that music you've been wanting. If you stay consistent all month, choose rewards that are fun and unusual yet in harmony with the hero you're becoming.

"Learn from yesterday, live for today, hope for tomorrow."
-Albert Einstein

As the next month nears, start preparing your Celebration and New Month's Resolutions. If something didn't work last month, no problem! Try something new this time. Your goal is not perfection, but building the habit of rising every time you stumble. Show yourself the love and mercy you would show others. Improve each month, and find joy along the way—design a heroic life!

Here's an example of what your New Month Resolutions may look like for love.

Theme For This New Month: Water Dragon!

Love
Primary Goal: To play with my partner in water in a way that is both joyful and healing.
Primary Avoidance: Fights. We will take time before traveling to breathe together as we embrace.

Days 1-10
Goals: Have a relaxing salt bath, swim in the ocean twice, and walk in the river once.
Rewards: New diving fins.

New Month Resolutions

Date: _____ / _____ / _____

Theme For This New Month: _____

Love
Primary Goal:

Primary Avoidance:

Health
Primary Goal:

Primary Avoidance:

Meaning
Primary Goal:

Primary Avoidance:

Wealth
Primary Goal:

Primary Avoidance:

Happiness
Primary Goal:

Primary Avoidance:

What Will Provide Love This Month

Days 1-10
Goals:
Rewards:
Days 11-20
Goals:
Rewards:
Days 21-On
Goals:
Rewards:

What Will Provide Health This Month

Days 1-10
Goals:
Rewards:
Days 11-20
Goals:
Rewards:
Days 21-On
Goals:
Rewards:

What Will Provide Meaning This Month

Days 1-10
Goals:
Rewards:
Days 11-20
Goals:
Rewards:
Days 21-On
Goals:
Rewards:

What Will Provide Wealth This Month
Days 1-10
Goals:
Rewards:
Days 11-20
Goals:
Rewards:
Days 21-On
Goals:
Rewards:

What Will Provide Happiness This Month
Days 1-10
Goals:
Rewards:
Days 11-20
Goals:
Rewards:
Days 21-On
Goals:
Rewards:

Print this off, and record memories on the back from the New Month Festival you celebrated, along with reflections on what did and didn't work well last month. Then begin a New Month's Resolution.

Introspection

The following section has been criticized by early readers, therapists, editors, and, well, everyone so far. "You can't say that! Don't use that word! Delete this example! It doesn't even fit!" But I stand by it as something that helped me early in my journey. If early, why is this placed so late in the workbook and series? Because we are still drafting our hero, and since this is a draft, and drafts get revised—not once, but as often as you sit down to examine it with introspection (which is the key to it all)—I've chosen to place this unorthodox measure here.

"Let us consider that we are all partially insane.
It will explain us to each other; it will unriddle many riddles;
it will make clear and simple many things which are involved
in haunting and harassing difficulties and obscurities now."
-Mark Twain

That fellow in the insane asylum who thinks he's Napoleon? Well, he really does think he is Napoleon! To him, he is sane. You aren't!

While you may not think you are Napoleon, can you say with certainty that you are 100% sane? Does *anyone* possess perfect thinking *or* feeling? Have you ever known something to be true, good, and beneficial, but then did the opposite?

Voltaire's famous saying, "Common sense is not too common." has one major flaw: common people never think it applies to them.

Many years ago, doctors would work on sick people or even at the morgue, and then deliver a baby without washing their hands, only to wonder why so many babies died. Dr. Ignaz Semmelweis discovered that washing his hands would save lives. He shared his findings and other doctors found it effective, but since the medical profession deemed such a thing as lunacy, this doctor was placed in an insane asylum where he was beaten to death by guards.

Washing your hands was not yet common sense (Louis Pasteur proved this to be true only a few years later). In today's society, men have traded morality for popularity, ethics for virtue-signaling, and the dapperness it takes to open the door for any lady (or for a lady to allow him) for nothing at all—we have just lost basic manners! We lost common sense. And just as the invisible bacteria on the unwashed hands of the doctors spread disease, unseen viruses—such as pornography, violent programming (read that last word again), and a general apathy toward our own physical, mental, and spiritual health—fester within us. We have not washed our hearts, but it is our responsibility to do so!

"We do not have to visit a madhouse to find disordered minds; our planet is the mental institution of the universe."
-Johann Wolfgang von Goethe

Too metaphysical? Albert Einstein said, "We cannot solve our problems with the same level of thinking that created them." Becoming aware of our nonsense is difficult without outside help. Like ships in drawn-out war, we have detectors altering us to the enemies outside, but no sensors altering us to the enemies inside. For this, older tools must be used: Tarot. Elders. Dreams. ... Pain. What needs changed? Poverty of income and mind? In fear, we often shift blame or workload onto others. There is, however, a way that works:

Change vs. Awakening

𝒜 simple way to look at change is with diet. A person who knows her breakfast is not healthy may switch to a different one, but without an inner awakening, she will easily revert to old habits.

Now consider someone who awakens. She sees factory farming firsthand, a friend of hers is dying from cancer, and she reads about what her diet is doing to her mind. She now sees how, not just inhumane, but inhuman the meat industry is, and cravings cannot compel her to pay for another pack of cigarettes—not with cash, but with years taken from her life. She also can no longer eat corn syrups and processed fats and still claim to have a mind, let alone love herself or those who care for her. She cannot live like that anymore! She has awakened. She does not force awakening on others, but she fully embraces her decision.

"The scientists of today think deeply instead of clearly.
One must be sane to think clearly, but one can
think deeply and be quite insane."
-Nikola Tesla

Change is a choice you could go back on. Awakening is a decision you won't go back on. Change is often due to popularity, convenience, or something you kind of want—or think you *should* want. Awakening is rooted in experiencing a great love or terrible pain, making it impossible to return to your former self. That said, awakening most often comes through painful life-altering circumstances thrust upon you, but it can also be sought out. Yet, even the bravest of us all tremble when peering into the mirror of our soul, our heart, our choices, and our habitual emotions.

The introspection required for drafting your hero and confronting your villain, demands asking daunting questions, such as: How many of those who condone spanking children would also condone slapping a husband or wife? How many of us who oppose suicide, unwittingly pursue it through the slower means of poor diet or legal drugs? Who among us would stand idly by if a stranger or our spouse were called names? Ah, but nearly all of us have called our loved ones' names, and we are all guilty of belittling a stranger a thousand-fold what we have seen others endure. That stranger we belittle? None other than ourselves.

Ask yourself:

Is it possible that there's something I don't understand?

What if understanding led to an awakening that would change everything for the better?

Would I pursue it?

Even if it was painful?

Albert Einstein also said, "Insanity is doing the same thing over and over again and expecting different results." We dream of being rich, loved, and happy—but our actions have not changed! Who is not guilty of this, even if unknowingly? Fixing unknown problems cannot be done alone; we must dig deep and seek assistance before we lose everything out of ignorance—or worse (and much more common), out of an unwillingness to face our problems.

One of the biggest problems? Anger.

While anger is one of the most destructive emotions, there are many kinds of anger: the kind that hits and the kind that gossips, the kind that erupts every week and the kind that is bottled up for years, ultimately destroying friendships and marriages when it explodes. We all have faults, and we must be brave enough to want to see them and correct them for the purpose of awakening.

In this, even the most well-off individuals should see a therapist and read *Hero, Vol. 3, H.A.L.T.—An Emotional Management Field Guide*.

No one goes through life without getting hurt, and our pains, no matter how much we think we can endure them, affect us and those around us. Those who do not seek help are often the ones who need it most. Do it, at the very least, for those you love.

Becoming the hero sounds scary. It is easier to stay the simple villain. What you have right now feels normal, and change, even if for the better, disrupts comfortable normalcy. Yet, here is the soothing truth and the scariest fact about change: it is going to happen anyway. Your life will change, but the person who recognizes this can guide that change for the better through the act of awakening.

To drive the point of awakening home, and to help find your partial insanity, consider this long quotation by Tony Robbins. Even if you don't like or agree with everything he says, I hope you underline parts of it anyway:

"If you question anything enough, eventually you will begin to doubt it. This is a tremendously effective strategy for shedding disempowering beliefs. I mean, haven't you done this with yourself? Aren't there areas in your life where you've doubted yourself? How'd you do it? You asked

yourself lousy questions like what if I screw up? What if I don't follow through? What if I forget what I'm supposed to do? And if you asked yourself enough of these questions then you began to doubt yourself. Why not use this force for good, and use it to destroy the limiting beliefs in your life? And as you question an old belief, it begins to build up evidence to support your new beliefs, ones that will empower you. Give it legs [like a table needs legs for support]. If you build up a belief enough, it will become something even stronger. It becomes a conviction. A conviction now is a belief that is reinforced by even more powerful references. It's an irresistible force for change. For example, let's say you decided never to eat meat again. To strengthen your resolve, talk to people who have chosen a vegetarian or vegan lifestyle. What reasons prompted them to change their diet, and what have been the consequences on their health and other areas of their life? What benefits have they received? In addition, begin to study the physiological impact that animal protein has on our bodies. The more references you develop, the more emotional these references are, the stronger your conviction will become. It becomes a conviction if you decide to go to a slaughterhouse and watch what's being destroyed in front of your very eyes, and what you're going to eat. I can promise you then, it will go from a belief you shouldn't do this, into a conviction that says, 'I couldn't consume this ever again!' Third, find a triggering event that will push you over the edge. Or else create one of your own, just as I've described."
-Tony Robbins

If a poet gets a job at a metalsmithing shop, or a metalsmith is tasked with writing, it does not matter how skilled the poet or metalsmith once was, the new task will be challenging and take time to grasp. So, too, is the process of changing a mindset of poverty into one of wealth.

When multimillionaires (provided they did not become wealthy through lottery or inheritance) lose their money, they often rebuild their fortune within a few years. Meanwhile, those who are poor and come into money—through a business or inheritance—often find themselves poorer within a few years. Money and wealth are products of a mindset focused on what can be achieved.

Anyone trying to improve their life will alter their diet and aim to improve their body's performance. And if they don't want to, but do so anyway—that is proof they are tired of being a victim to the bully of self.

To develop a new mindset of wealth, ask those two, five, and 10 years ahead of you exactly how they got there. Ask for their best advice, worst mistakes, and if they are still enjoying it. And those worse off? Ask them what distracts them from their goals—whether in love or business. Then, sit down with yourself and ask, "How did I get here? How easily could I fall? How can I achieve what I want—others have!—and be the person I long to be?"

"If you think anyone is sane,
you just don't know enough about them."
-Christopher Moore

To awaken, start by reading the best books on the other side of your current temporary views. Literally search for where you could be wrong. And when you find out you are wrong—bam!—now you know the truth and are right. How does this awakening help you? Now, when someone says something you disagree with, you recall that you disagree with your younger self. And since you are searching for where you may be in error, you know the future you will also disagree with the you of today. You are not upset with your younger self or afraid of growing, and this makes it easy to be at peace with different faiths and political views. The reward of enduring friendships built on respect costs only the price of a book and the courage to be wrong in order to be right.

Another method of awakening I learned by being around two people who embraced the fact that we will all die. They often reflected on this truth and spoke about it regularly—not with gloom, but with curiosity and humor. They realized that in a hundred years (likely less) no one would care if we wore the loud shirt we loved or were brave enough to tell a girl that we liked her, or even took a nap when we needed it. This perspective became their superpower. Their awakening to the inevitability of death gave them permission to fully live.

All of this has led me to stare out a window and dream of a book I have not read in many years—one that has changed so many lives. Let us dive even deeper into what has become merely a traditional movie or commonplace thought:

The Lifetimes Of Wisdom In Books

The theme of awakening, as well as the concept of wealth, is central to *A Christmas Carol,* by Charles Dickens. This story revolves around the miser, Scrooge, who worked others hard but worked himself harder. Scrooge had been hurt in the past, or "burned" as I call it—so he always treated people with coldness and contempt to protect himself from the pain of rejection. His bitter anger was a false power, as, for most of his life, he did not realize that his wall of defense was actually a prison of pain.

How do most of us escape from pain? We mentally retreat into the past, escape into the future, or numb ourselves in the present by running on autopilot emotions like anger. Scrooge's transformation began when he was visited by the Spirit of the Past, the Spirit of the Present, and the Spirit of the Future. He saw so much pain in the past—pain that steered him away from who he was—and even more pain in the present, magnified by the choices he had made. Then he saw horrible, unspeakable pain and death in the future—so much so that he could no longer pretend that all was well anymore. Scrooge awoke to the truth: the miser he had become was not who he truly was. He was not the mask-wearing villain who suffocated his true identity, but the heart-wearing hero who spread cheer and joy.

"I don't think we spend enough time in reflection and introspection. We don't know who we are as individuals in this culture anymore."
-Naomi Judd

Spirit Of The Past

To continue your journey of introspection, find a spot in nature with no distractions, allowing peaceful privacy. Once there, reflect on the root of an issue in your life. Look back with the Spirit of the Past to identify a time before this problem existed. In *A Christmas Carol,* Scrooge revisits the moment just before he deviated. He could see the cheerful man he used to be. Only then could he see where he stopped being himself and started carrying pain—but that pain was so overwhelming that he masked it with bitterness. Others cover pain or fear with overt happiness, gluttony, greed, or rage.

"All of humanity's problems stem from man's inability to sit quietly in a room alone."
-Blaise Pascal

Psychologists ask many questions to uncover these roots because, once you find them, everything changes. Sometimes, battling anxiety head-on yields no results, but finding the root can vanquish half the struggle in a single moment!

If you get anxiety around five every evening, and it gets worse as the night progresses, think back to when this wasn't the case. Indeed, you may have to ask other people or delve deeply into your memories. You were not like this when you were four. At that little school, you were fine. After you moved, everything was wonderful for years. Your new stepdad, though, always got home at five, didn't he? He was not very nice to you, and you worried about your mom's safety, as well as your own. That was 40 years ago.

A young man who is struggling with depression may upset his friends with constant self-deprecating remarks, leaving them tired of reassuring him. After weeks of looking into the past, he realizes the root isn't from when he was six or four, but before he was born. His mom and dad both could not love themselves so they had other people do it for them, his mom used pity, and his dad used work. The young man realizes at once he seeks praise by making negative comments about himself and, despite years of being praised for his work ethic, feels worthless the moment he sits down. While now his journey of seeking self-love and self-worth begins, he knows that his foundation is not his own—these do not belong to him. It is an inheritance he can reject.

Seeing work as a joy rather than a trade, this person now begins to see that earned rest doesn't make anyone worthless. And if we have loved ones, by default it means we are lovable, and questioning our worth is questioning their value as well. We must not do this to ourselves or others. While the woman may always become a little anxious at five, understanding the cause lets her reclaim control. She can say, "No. I am safe. And I love myself enough to not hate myself or get more anxious about this anxiety."

From genetics to emulating an old friend, finding the source is one of the greatest tools in life. Identifying the roots helps you heal in ways no other method can.

"It is necessary now and then for a man to go away by himself and experience loneliness; to sit on a rock in the forest and to ask of himself, 'Who am I, and where have I been, and where am I going?' ... If one is not careful, one allows diversions to take up one's time—the stuff of life."
-Carl Sandburg

A famous line among therapists is, "Tell me about your mother." And that is a good place to start, unless you do so with blame in your heart. Each of us has traits from our families; however, we do not have to keep the ones we dislike, and we can cultivate any missing ones we desire. We are new architects of a building that has already been built.

> *"In order to understand the world,*
> *one has to turn away from it on occasion."*
> *-Albert Camus*

You might ask, "Why do I think it is funny to X?" You then look deeply at your past for the places where this behavior (good or bad) originated. Let's say it came from your brother. You then ask, "Why do I choose to emulate him? Is there someone I would rather emulate?" As you go, dive deep with questions like, "If I could alter three things about how my parents raised me, what would they be—and how can I raise myself now by doing just that?" Even smaller questions such as, "Why do I enjoy drinking tea alone?" can lead you to profound self-discovery as you seek all the similar things you like to do alone because ... well, because of what?

As the Spirit of the Past guides you, remember that your goal is to be better, not beaten, bitter, or to blame. We are not visiting the past to blame others and hold the world's largest pity party where only one person shows up (yourself), or the world's smallest pity party, where only one person shows up (yourself). We seek to identify where it is we diverged—to find the wealth of inner peace.

Spirit Of The Present

I've known Christian men who love their wives more than their own lives, as the Bible commands. Yet these good men listen to society tell them they are toxic, so they do not love themselves. And so their love for others was dim, but even dim lights seem bright in the dark.

We seldom visit the Spirit of the Present, choosing instead to linger in the past or dream of the future, never pausing to know that right now shall be the past, and is indeed the future we have dreamed of.

Look at where you are. Take an honest inventory. You got here. You are here. This reveals what kind of life you believed you deserve. Many still have boxes filled with old things, not as keepsakes or things we haven't gotten to yet, but because we secretly long to go back home. Some of us have great jobs and wonderful friends, but live in squalor and treat our bodies like trashcans. Others tend to their only home (their bodies) but work a job that is killing them. Many of us are punishing ourselves today for the crimes of yesterday, with the biggest one being that of our dreams unfulfilled.

*"The deeper I go into myself
the more I realize that I am my own enemy."*
-Floriano Martins

Tiny Tim, in *A Christmas Carol*, was in great need, but Scrooge couldn't see it. Who has a need in your life? And don't overlook this! It is so easy to see it in other people, yet so challenging to see it in ourselves. Who has a need that you are ignoring? Even if it is yours, dare to look closely.

Once or twice a year, I sit and look at what I've achieved. I remind myself of how far I've come and feel grateful for my hard work. I also see where friendships are fading, or someone needs my help. Sometimes, to truly be present (as simple as this is), you have to stop long enough to look. Try it for yourself right now. Not for a mere moment. Take your time and look at here and now.

> *"'But you were always a good man of business, Jacob,'*
> *faltered Scrooge, who now began to apply this to himself.*
> *'Business!' cried the Ghost, wringing its hands again.*
> *'Mankind was my business; charity, mercy, forbearance,*
> *and benevolence, were all my business. The deals of*
> *my trade were but a drop of water in the*
> *comprehensive ocean of my business!'"*
> *-Charles Dickens*

Spirit Of The Future

Write what you want in life, so long as it aligns with what would be good for you, and what would be good for others in the short and long term.

This may sound like something to skip, but if you spell out what you want and treat aiming at and moving towards those goals (not the goals themselves) as the goal and joy of life itself, then you'll find joy in life itself. Goals move as you move, and we need more goals when we reach one or change our trajectory. Knowing this helps make life worth enduring. If you wait to be happy until you've "made it," well, you'll never make it (since there are always new goals) so why bother going at all? But if your happiness lies in pursuing a meaningful life, then happiness can be yours right now, and it will grow, not due to achievement, but due to self-love.

"If you can't forgive and forget, pick one."
-Robert Brault

Do not dream aimlessly of the future while neglecting the present. When looking at life in the present, ask yourself, "Is this where I thought I'd be five years ago?" Few can answer yes because few change the habitual systems that guide their trajectory. You do not need to change your dreams, but you must change your methods.

When I drafted my villain in *Hero, Vol. 1*, it terrified me. I knew destruction could happen with little effort. It would be easy for alcohol to ruin my life, to lose friends by shunning them for having different views, or to forgo passions by obeying my depression. By evoking the Spirit of the Future, we bring a pen to a sword fight!

Once more, look at where you are today, and envision things as being much worse. You are drinking more (or maybe even less), and it costs your license and a friend in a car accident. You are more slovenly, and the mess around you catches on fire. You haven't improved your diet at all, and now your pain has become unbearable and so you have no choice but to quit your job and rely on others. But you do have a choice. The Spirit of the Future can look in your window and see you pouring your drinks down the drain. It can see you cleaning the house and giving to those in need, and though you could have sworn the wind sounded like laughter, you are nonetheless exercising in a way that makes you happy. What, then, does the future look like? Could it be that being sober is better than you ever surmised? Could it be that being healthy and fit doesn't just save your job or your life, but the life of someone in need? Could it be? Could the future be as bright as you paint it, no matter how dark the frame of life is?

"It is good to love many things,
for therein lies the true strength,
and whosoever loves much performs much,
and can accomplish much,
and what is done in love is well done."
-Vincent Van Gogh

War is coming. Loved ones will die. Jobs will be lost. Friends, even lovers, will stab you in the back. And hope will be the fog of fantasy or a heavy truth made manifest through work. Let us make the art we have always wanted to. Let us become heroes, even if that means we one day come home on our shields. For we will, nonetheless, come home.

Our Spirit Of Looking

Scrooge was rich the day before the spirits visited. He was wealthy thereafter by giving.

The pathway towards wealth you are drafting is about more than mere money. Write five things that are causing you emotional pain. Keep it as short as possible, such as: "I yell at my husband." or, "My house is a mess."

1.

2.

3.

4.

5.

You may start with, "I yelled at my husband," but if left unchecked for a year, it could lead to the loss of marriage, the compounded pain of a death, the unexpected leaving of a friend, or even being arrested. Be honest—not lovingly honest or brutally honest—just honest. Under each of your previous answers, write one line about what you see through the lens of the Spirit of the Past, the Spirit of the Present, and the Spirit of the Future.

What events can awaken you? Seek them! Literally find what will cause these emotional pains to no longer have a place to stay in your home. Look at them closely and visit them with 10 times the effort you think is needed. To where it is uncomfortable? No. Scrooge was not uncomfortable. He was terrified!

We often try to push ordinary people to become extraordinary, but that approach will never work—people have to pull themselves up the ladder of improvement, otherwise, you will wear yourself out trying to improve others, never knowing how much you could improve your ordinary self! And that—that alone!—will help guide others more than anything else.

"Action is a great restorer and builder of confidence.
Inaction is not only the result, but the cause, of fear.
Perhaps the action you take will be successful;
perhaps different action or adjustments will have
to follow. But any action is better than no action at all."
-Norman Vincent Peale

How do you inflict the necessary pain to elicit your own desire to awaken? Walking a long trail for weeks, going without food for days, praying in the woods for long periods, and visiting a third-world country? All good places for introspection. Attend classes you don't want to, or think you don't need, such as ones on domestic violence, presentations on drunk driving, seminars for business, courses on parenting, and workshops on intimacy. These resources are not just for those in crisis—I wish every non-drinker knew how to combat cravings for alcohol, and just how much it could cost. The world would only improve if those who did not have children learned how to lovingly raise them. If I could teach only one thing, it would be how to love others—for to properly love others, we must also love ourselves.

Seek, learn, and suffer now, so you do not suffer much worse later. Today, not tomorrow, write out your New Month's Resolutions. Where will you seek the teacher known as Pain? Write how you will awaken. You can aim, or you can be aimless.

"There is no coming to consciousness without pain."
-Carl Jung

Introspection is like wisdom, it is wonderful in moderation, but too much can bring unnecessary sorrow. Play, laugh, and smile more than you study. We need both play and wisdom, or our joy will be stolen.

However, allow others to grow in their own way. If you want to help them, focus on improving yourself. Offer praise for every step they take, no matter how small or rare. Cheer if they pass you; give a standing ovation if they stand back up— even if only to stumble again.

Giving

There are no stories about a happy miser. Hoarders are portrayed as crazy. The common expression is that giving is its own reward, but many scowl at the idea simply because they don't know how to give.

Let's say you've saved 10% of your income for charity over the last few months, and you now have $1,000. Granted, you could send a check to an organization. That is fine. Or perhaps you could treat it like a personal investment and do this instead:

You buy $900 worth of blankets (or anything—hats, paintings, coffee, tools—you name it) from a group that employs those rescued from prostitution, those who are homeless, veterans who have found it difficult to find employment, or anyone you resonate with. Of these items, you keep something for yourself and take the rest to a local humane society, orphanage, or homeless food kitchen, and you donate these items to their fundraiser auction. In doing this, you helped the people you bought these items from, were kind to yourself and enjoyed one of the items, supported the fundraiser with needed income, and highlighted the value this other charity offers, too.

"Your wealth is not defined by your capacity to accumulate, rather by your capacity to give away."
-Manoj Arora

And that extra $100? You invest it in yourself by buying healthier food or a book that could help you become a better employee, increasing your income and allowing you to do this noble and enjoyable act again in a few weeks or months.

From buying a group of volunteers lunch to taking the day off and helping them clean up the beach, giving back to the community (Earth) you live in, enriches the lives of those around you. And there is no way to escape it: you enrich your own life as well, and *that* is buying wealth with money.

> *"I slept and dreamt that life was joy.*
> *I awoke and saw that life was service.*
> *I acted and behold, service was joy."*
> *-Rabindranath Tagore*

Write at least four people or places you would like to support. Then decide what percent of your total income you will donate to them. No excuses! Even if you were to become homeless, donate a portion of what you receive from charity to a charity. Even if you have no money, find a way to donate a percentage of your time. Without doing this, no amount of money would avail you the true riches of life.

1.
2.
3.
4.

> *"Life is so subtle that sometimes you*
> *barely notice yourself walking through*
> *the doors you once prayed would open."*
> *-Brianna Wiest*

Life without gratitude is devoid of grace. Even if you are homeless, lonely, or ill, focus on gratitude. Start now and never stop.

Write a dozen uncommon things you are grateful for. From being able to wiggle your toes to the scent of air after it rains, from your grandmother's love for barn dances to a card you received 20 years ago—when we practice unorthodox gratitude, we will have unorthodox grace.

1.
2.
3.
4.
5.
6.
7.
8.
9.
10.
11.
12.

If you want money—the amount you discovered in the beginning—then follow the principles in this book.

Start!

But if you also want wealth, share your gratitude with others every day. Take a moment right now and reach out to the people you are thankful for.

"Do you remember those days? Do you remember dreaming about being a champion, making a difference, making history? Don't we all dream about making our family proud? To some extent, we all want to be heroes. We have a desire to deliver for our loved ones, the ones who count on us, to earn their love and respect. Hollywood makes money by creating movies to make us believe for a split second that we can be Rocky, Rudy, Patton, or Alexander the Great. The downside is that we spend time and money to watch that hero instead of being that hero ourselves."
-Patrick Bet-David

On her shirt is a note saying "Pity The Blind."
Do not let your wealth go by unnoticed — from seeing a
rainbow to hearing music. — Silly, I know, but I often wish I
could step into this painting and provide.

217

Wealth

It is late in the writing of this book, mere days before I send it off for editing. Still, after talking to my blind uncles, visiting with brothers at dance, and shooting the breeze with cowboys at the vineyard where I work, I wanted to add a bit more about wealth and a lot less about money.

Right now, I am sitting, and writing (obvious, perhaps, but it's what I love to do), and before me stretches acres of budding vines, purple and white irises in bloom, red leaves of roses just peeking out, rabbits playing in the foyer, and, softly, new songs by Tobias Tinker fill the air. It is calm. I am alone but not lonely. I am rich beyond measure.

A few weeks ago, I house-sat a beautiful home in the mountains, far away from anyone. As I took care of the horses, there were elk, turkeys, rabbits, ravens, and coyotes playing about. The muse whispered as I wrote amidst wind, snowstorms, rain complete with rainbows, and sunny days, all of which visited during those two weeks. I was paid to housesit, where others would have spent many thousands to stay there, but the wealth was not the money, it was nature. It was the nurturing peace of wildlife, trees, and the untamed rhythm of the weather. It was in not hearing traffic or people for weeks. I could not have been richer had I owned the mountains themselves.

In winter, while in a tropical region, I vividly recall laughing as I floated in the ocean, looking up at green mountains and food forests along the banks of the pale blue calm and calming waters. There was no ticket booth. This place—this experience—was free. That same morning, on another beach, I watched a sea turtle emerge from the ocean and slowly approach a woman sitting on a log. As I walked along, in love with the mountainous backdrop, sunrise, rainbow in the distant rain, and tranquility of it all, I unabashedly approached the woman with a smile and said, "No amount of money could ever buy this." She smiled sweetly as she snuggled her hot coffee and whispered, "I know." I walked away, finding shells and so many gratitudes along the beach that fine morning. And dear reader, during winter, I live here. This—this!—is free.

Wealth—ask anyone who has lost theirs—yes, wealth is time spent with mother, skills learned from father, cookies baked by grandmother, and tales shared by grandfather. It is a kiss on the cheek, a second glance from a woman, and the way community comes together during a catastrophe to love and help one another even more.

Money? Sure. I once bought a woman I loved deeply a Nordic dress, and I recall her wearing it on a long trip we took. There was a moment when she was smelling lilacs for the first time in perhaps decades. I will never forget the ethereal smile in her eyes as the light glistened on the grass like glass hanging in a window.

I miss her.

But this, too, is wealth.

Choosing to be hurt—or bravery, as I call it—is better than choosing to be bitter, living in want of the past or denying a possible future.

From petting kittens in a coffee shop with a dear friend to telling a stranger she has beautiful eyes, from thanking a veteran who says, behind eyes about to weep, that I needn't thank him, to watching a bat clean herself—these moments are true wealth. I once planted heirloom plum trees (the same ones that inspired the sugar plum fairy stories), and one evening I saw one plum had gone bad. I was about to pluck it off when I realized it was actually a little brown bat. I got a bucket and sat a ways away, watching the bat wake, lick her wings, stretch, and yawn—so many big yawns. Then, all at once, she let go and glided away without a sound. I spent an hour doing that for free. A video would not do it justice.

Entertainment? I do not remember most of it—but I recall feeding blue jays and barn swallows at a wildlife rehab, helping perform surgery on a tiger at a wildlife sanctuary, and working with vets to deliver ponies and calves. I remember the time a fox sat beside me, a coyote walked with me, and when my favorite pets died in my hands ... Love has always made me wealthy, even when it walks away—even when death comes.

I could make more money working a job I hate, but there is so much work that is wonderful—hard and stressful at times, but wonderful. With free time, I could see a show, and I do on occasion, but real wealth is the ability to share a homegrown and homemade meal, an adventure unplanned, and a dance with loved ones you just met, all while growing more and more in love with yourself. Even a walk in a park, planting tulip bulbs, or working on a car with a brother— these are all pure wealth.

I would never wish to give up my wealth for money. And with the money I make, I have zero regrets about spending it on the adventure of life. Be wealthy, my friends. Even if, for a time, you are poor in money.

"I want, what they want, and every other guy who came over here and spilled his guts and gave everything he had, wants! For our country to love us as much as we love it! That's what I want!"
-Rambo

To Close

At the beginning of this, we made a deal: that you would give 10% of your extra income to charity. To be imperatively repetitive: if you adhere to this honor system, only then will you be wealthy. Not because of karma or the like, but because the maxim, "It's better to give than to receive." is absolute truth and the flower of wealth.

"There is no time for cut-and-dried monotony.
There is time for work.
And time for love.
That leaves no other time."
-Coco Chanel

Being wealthy is not found in hoarding or poverty. Wealth is not found in being taken advantage of or sacrificing ideals, passions, and family.

Wealth?

Wealth is supporting groups of men who fight against sex trafficking, be it girls being sold or pornography of women acting like little girls for free—enslaving the minds by capturing the souls of both user and used.

Wealth is food for the starving stranger who is eager to work. Wealth is medicine. Wealth is being able to take time off and restore a beach with groups who love the sea— meeting wonderful people who are so similar yet so vastly different. It's the nature, the waves, the strangers turned friends, the laughter of children, the sea turtle you spotted, and the fish jumping in the surf—yes, *that* is wealth.

Wealth is hearing the words, "I love you." even if it took 10 years to find, a year to lose, and another five years to find again and keep thus far.

Wealth is hearing grandfather share stories about the most wonderful things grandmother has done for him, as well as his hardships in the war. Those tears are invaluable!

Wealth is freedom, liberty, and joy in the pursuit of your ideal. But make sure you share that joy, and allow others their joy, too.

"Life had gotten too busy.
It seemed as if my existence had
become just one long to-do list. I had
forgotten about my dreams, my goals,
my what-ifs, my 'what if I could's.'"
-Amy Haines

If you apply the tools herein, then you will have money. But if you continue to improve your life through this series, then a charitable, honorable, and noble hero will have wealth. When this happens, the world is blessed by your talents and shines a little brighter because of you. To find even greater wealth—perhaps the greatest of all—continue your journey by reading and applying *Hero, Vol. 5: Relationships: Finding One, Being In One, & Parting Ways*.

—Raven

"And the day came when the risk to remain tight in a bud
was more painful than the risk it took to blossom."
-Anaïs Nin

"Be so good they can't ignore you."
-Steve Martin

A Final Note

By starting and not stopping, by learning as you go—not before you go!—*this* creates income. To do what we love, at least most of the time, and to care for ourselves and others—*this* is wealth.

I so want you to succeed in life. Every wonderful meal, work of art, road I drive on, and song I dance to was the hard work and dream of another. I am thankful for their success, and I hope earnestly for yours. It is not selling out, but a gift to us all!

In this, may you stumble your way forward and enjoy it so much that the stumbling goes unnoticed. May you be wealthy—so wealthy that your richness enhances the lives of everyone around you. Like light, sharing this knowledge does not diminish your money or your wealth. So I hope you will share this book and encourage others to read the works of this series. To further your wealth, explore all the books, join the newsletter, and enjoy free worksheets, go to:

www.emotionalmanagement.org

"You can only become truly
accomplished at something you love.
Don't make money your goal.
Instead pursue the things you love doing
and then do them so well that
people can't take their eyes off of you."
-Maya Angelou

About The Author

Raven is a viticulturist (fancy word for farmer), author (obsessive tinkering disorder), women's self-defense instructor with 35+ years of teaching experience (proficient in Ninjutsu, Tae Kwon Do, and Tai Chi Chuan), volunteers at wildlife rehabilitation centers and sanctuaries (a keeper of all things wild), and dances ecstatically (battling inner demons, and outer ones too, always with hints of playfulness, love, and gratitude).

His qualifications to write these workbooks:

Raven's family has gone through hard times; indeed, he went from being homeless to having a life many are jealous of, not because of fancy cars, which he doesn't own, but because of the life he lives and the epic friends he has. But more than being often found in libraries and bookshops, more than a dusty diploma proving something was memorized for a test 30 years ago, Raven's real qualification is that he's stubborn. Staying with the questions longer, listening to Elders and dreams, he brings about in his words uncommon ideas. The most uncommon of all? Rather than guiding you, Raven's only goal is to help you guide yourself.

"If you light a lamp for someone else,
it will also brighten your path."
-Buddha

The Lovers

I would give all my money to be with loved ones lost
Yes, some have fancy cars, amusements, and big houses
But others have gold, seeds, and a large, loving family

You're no sell-out or con-artist — but a provider, a hero!
What you give this world is a gift that gives back
Wealth is time with loved ones, and passions pursued

Do not give up, least of all before you try. Start!

Made in the USA
Monee, IL
08 March 2025

13415252R00128